THE
RIGHT
TO SILENCE

THE
RIGHT
TO SILENCE

Privileged Clergy
Communication
and the Law

WILLIAM HAROLD TIEMANN AND JOHN C. BUSH

Abingdon Press
Nashville

THE RIGHT TO SILENCE
PRIVILEGED CLERGY COMMUNICATION AND THE LAW

Originally published as The Right to Silence: Privileged Communication and the Pastor. © *M. E. Bratcher 1964*

Second edition, revised and updated, copyright © 1983 by Abingdon Press

Library of Congress Cataloging in Publication Data

TIEMANN, WILLIAM HAROLD
    The right to silence.
    Includes bibliographical references and indexes.
    1. Confidential communications—Clergy—United States.
    2. Confidential communications—Clergy.
    I. Bush, John C., 1938-   II. Title.
    KF8959.C6T5   1983   347.73'66   83-6401
                                347.30766

ISBN 0-687-36315-2

Scripture quotations unless otherwise noted are from the Revised Standard Version of the Bible, copyrighted 1946, 1952, 1971, © 1973, by the Division of Christian Education of the National Council of the Churches of Christ in the U.S.A., and used by permission.

Those indicated KJV are from the King James Version of the Bible.

The quotation on pages 180-81 is an excerpt from the article: "'Tell All' or Go to Jail: A Dilemma for the Clergy" by Dean M. Kelley. Copyright 1974 Christian Century Foundation. Reprinted by permission from the January 30, 1974, issue of The Christian Century/The Christian Ministry.

MANUFACTURED BY THE PARTHENON PRESS AT
NASHVILLE, TENNESSEE, UNITED STATES OF AMERICA

CONTENTS

PREFACE TO
THE SECOND EDITION

In the nineteen years since this book first appeared under
the title: *The Right to Silence* (John Knox Press, 1964), many
changes have occurred in the legal status of clergy keeping
confidences. Originally, thirty-seven states had statutes
guaranteeing this privilege to a greater or lesser extent.
Now there are forty-nine. Then, the privilege was quite
strictly construed to mean mostly or always "penitential"
communications; now, with the 1974 recommendations of
the Supreme Court to broaden the statutes on privilege,
confidential communications of many kinds are recognized
in the federal court system and often by the states as well.
(While Congress did not approve the specific Supreme
Court recommendations, it did allow for a case-by-case
definition of privileged communication and the high court's
recommendations have often been used as guidelines.)

Also, as predicted, many more cases of this kind have
been before the courts in recent years. The expansion of the
role of pastoral counseling, the active support and
participation of the clergy in the militant activities of the
sixties and seventies, the alleged use by the CIA of American
missionaries overseas as spies and informers, the rise of the
drug culture in this country and elsewhere—all these have
involved clergy in counseling and chaplaincy activities

where they have knowledge which, to some, would make them competent witnesses in civil and criminal cases. Hence, there has been a need to update this book and expand its scope.

John Bush has been responsible for several new chapters and additional material on some of the original ones. In addition, it is his interest and impetus that caused this book to receive a second life. William Tiemann has been responsible for additional material on several of the old chapters, for a complete revision of all chapters to remove sexist language, and for an update of the legal status of clergy on these issues. In addition, he had the responsibility of overall editor and compiler of all material.

If this book is helpful to clergy in their relations to the courts of the land, our purpose will have been served.

William Harold Tiemann
John C. Bush

PREFACE TO
THE FIRST EDITION

Just after lunch the phone rang at the manse. I answered. It was the county sheriff—he had received a subpoena for me; would I come to his office and accept it? A few minutes later I knew the details.

Sometime before, I had counseled extensively with a couple contemplating divorce. When the breakup of the marriage seemed imminent, I had suggested that they place their two children in a denominational children's home, since neither would be able to care for them. They had done this when they separated. Now, months later, one of the parties sought to gain the full custody of the children. On the basis of a case study, the children's home refused. A court action ensued. I was being subpoenaed as a witness for the children's home. My testimony was to help sustain the home's refusal to give up custody of the children.

I accepted the subpoena because there seemed little else to do. But I felt I could never testify in this case. Everything I knew about the couple had been told me in the confidence of the pastor's study. My opinion given to the court would be breaking this trust. There was no other way to look at it honestly. Of course, I was concerned about the children. But there were other ways the court could get the information necessary to make a decision. What seemed important now was my right—in fact, my necessity as a pastor—to keep silent. Violation of a personal confidence seemed a grave error. But could the court force me to testify?

In apprehension, I placed a long distance call to my seminary's professor of practical theology. "What are my rights?" I asked him. Was there a book I could refer to? There was no book, but his counsel was sage: "Go to a lawyer you trust, lay ten dollars on his desk and ask his advice." The lawyer—a friend—refused the ten dollars but was generous with his advice. When the case came to trial, I did not testify.

My interest in the subject of a pastor's right to silence began with this incident. An opportunity to do graduate study provided the time for research for this book. While its cost is not much more than ten dollars, this text is not meant to take the place of a lawyer's counsel. But within these pages, a pastor may find the answer to those questions which will determine whether he should search out a lawyer for specific advice. Most ministers know little or nothing about their legal right to receive and hold confessions and confidences. Perhaps these chapters can serve as a primer in an unfamiliar area.

Many persons have helped bring this book together. Especially important have been those pastors with experiences similar to my own who have graciously shared their counsel with me. Acknowledgment of each is made later in the text. Special thanks should go to the administrators and staff of the libraries of these institutions: the Austin Presbyterian Theological Seminary, the Perkins School of Theology and the School of Law at Southern Methodist University, the Supreme Court of the State of Texas, and the School of Law at the University of Texas. Their assistance was always thoughtful and most helpful. For much encouragement, some criticism, and many suggestions, I am grateful to President David Stitt and Professors

Henry W. Quinius, Jr., Prescott H. Williams, Jr., and Charles L. King at the Austin Presbyterian Seminary. John Plath Green of Lefkowitz, Green, Ginsberg, Eades, and Gilmore, Dallas, has given these pages legal respectability and the author many enlightening hours interpreting courtroom terminology and procedure. Miss Adele Acrey, Mrs. Dan Gleckler, Mrs. John Solomon, and my wife have, over several years, patiently typed and retyped the preliminary and final manuscripts. Members of the staff of John Knox Press have been of great help in putting everything together in proper form for publication. The errors that remain are my own; the credit for any correctness must be shared with everyone above. Finally, acknowledgment should be made of the staff and saints at Preston Hollow Presbyterian Church, Dallas, who never once complained that the associate pastor was spending too much time writing a book and neglecting his work. He was—but their understanding was boundless.

W. H. T.

For everything there is a season, and a time for every matter under heaven . . . a time to keep silence, and a time to speak.
Ecclesiastes 3:1, 7

I have often regretted my speech, never my silence.
Publilius Syrus, *circa* 42 B.C.

Part I/THE
CHURCHES AND
CONFIDENTIALITY

Chapter 1/WHY IS THERE A PROBLEM?

May 14, 1981. The Reverend Ron Salfen, a Presbyterian minister, stood before the bench of State District Judge John Roach in the courthouse at McKinney, Texas. He had a choice to make and, regardless of what he decided, he had a price to pay. His choice was between obedience to his calling as a minister and obedience to an order of the court. He chose the former. Judge Roach gave Salfen an indefinite jail sentence for contempt of court.

The minister had appeared as a character witness for his secretary in a bond hearing. Under cross-examination by the prosecutor he was asked questions about matters he had discussed with the woman in confidence. Citing the Texas clergy-penitent statute, he declined to reveal anything told to him in this confidential conversation. There were six questions and six refusals to break the seal of confidentiality.

And so Ron Salfen stood before Judge Roach, who repeated each of the six questions, each of which stood as a separate charge of contempt of court. To each question, the reply was the same: "I'm sorry, your honor, I cannot answer."

Judge Roach found the pastor guilty on all six counts of contempt, assessed a fine of a hundred dollars for each count plus a sentence of twelve hours in jail on each charge, and ordered him held in jail until he was willing to answer the questions put to him by the court.

After the sentencing, the judge told the minister, "This court is not mad at you. I just expect my orders to be obeyed."

Happily, it took the Texas Court of Criminal Appeals only five hours to order the minister released, and at a hearing two weeks later that court overruled Judge Roach on the contempt citations.[1] Still, the experience of Dr. Salfen was unpleasant, distasteful, and heartrending for the pastor, his family, his congregation, and his fellow clergy in Texas. But his experience is not unique. It is only the most recent in a centuries-long battle for the right to silence.

Regina versus Hay—A Classic Case. One of the more interesting cases in this long battle took place in England in 1860 in the court of his Lordship, Mr. Justice Hill.

William Hay was charged with robbing Daniel Kennedy of a silver watch at Jarrow on Christmas Day 1859. Inspector Rogers apprehended Hay, and from information provided by Hay the inspector went to the house of the Reverend John Kelley, a Roman Catholic priest. Here he received a watch which Mr. Kennedy identified as his property.

At the trial, Father Kelley was called as a witness for the prosecution, but when the crier of the court was about to administer the oath to him the priest objected to its form. The following exchange took place:

His Lordship: What is the objection?

Witness: Not that I shall tell the truth, and nothing but the truth; but as a minister of the Catholic Church, I object to the part that states that I shall tell the whole truth.

His Lordship: The meaning of the oath is this: it is the whole truth touching the trial which you are asked; which you, legitimately according to law, can be asked. . . . You can therefore have no objection as a loyal subject, and in duty to the laws of the country, to answer the whole truth touching the case which may be lawfully asked. Therefore you must be sworn.

The witness took the oath in its usual form and gave the following evidence:

Witness: I have been twelve years Catholic priest at the Felling. On Christmas Day I received the watch produced.

Prosecutor: From whom did you receive that watch?

Witness: I received it in connection with the confessional.

His Lordship: You are not asked at present to disclose anything stated to you in the confessional; you are asked a simple fact—from whom did you receive that watch which you gave to the policeman?

Witness: The reply to that question would implicate the person who gave me the watch, therefore I cannot answer it. If I answered it, my suspension for life would be a necessary consequence. I should be violating the laws of the Church, as well as the natural laws.

His Lordship: I have already told you plainly I cannot enter into this question. All I can say is, you are bound to answer, "From whom did you receive that watch?" On the ground I have stated to you, you are not asked to disclose anything that a penitent may have said to you in the confessional. That you are not asked to disclose; but you are asked to disclose from whom you received stolen property on the 25th of December last. Do you answer it, or do you not?

Witness: I really cannot, my lord.

His Lordship: Then I adjudge you to be guilty of contempt of Court, and order you to be committed to gaol. *[To the officer of the Court]*—Take him into custody.

The witness was accordingly removed in custody and other witnesses were called.[2]

This case and many similar ones point up the problem

faced by ministers, priests, and rabbis, and in a somewhat different context by psychiatrists and mental health practitioners as well. To what extent are those confidences shared by parishioners and patients immune from disclosure in a court of law? Significant counseling can hardly take place when persons being counseled know that there is a possibility that their confidences may be made a matter of record in a civil or criminal case.

But how, under present statutes and court rulings, are such confessions protected from the ears of jury and judge? Perhaps some will decide that they should not be protected. There is historical basis for such a decision. But others feel differently, and with the increasing involved activity of the clergy in pastoral care and counseling the problems become more acute.

Canon Law and the Priest. This book deals with the issue of confidential communications as faced by minister, priest, and rabbi. In many ways the problems faced by each are the same, and to some degree they are shared by secular mental health practitioners as well. Yet there are distinct differences.

For the Roman Catholic priest confession is a sacrament, one of seven in the church. It is obligatory for Catholics to make confession to a priest. Under canon law the confession is inviolable, no matter what civil law says or does not say. Ecclesiastical law leaves no doubt about the action of a priest should a court require him to reveal knowledge gained through the confessional. The confessor cannot make revelation of confessional matter even in answer to false accusations by the confessant. The only way he can disclose anything learned in the course of confession is when the penitent freely and expressly gives the confessor permission to reveal it. Canon 889, section 1 reads: "The sacramental seal is inviolable, and hence the confessor shall be most careful not to betray the penitent by any word or sign or in any other way."[3]

Canon 2369 indicates the solemnity of the obligation. It provides that a confessor "who dares to break the seal of confession directly, remains under excommunication reserved *modo specialissimo* to the Apostolic See."[4]

The obligation of secrecy applies to anyone who obtains knowledge of the contents of a confession. Canon 889, section 2, says: "The obligation of keeping the sacramental seal binds also interpreters and all other persons who may in any way have acquired knowledge of confession."[5]

In effect, these canon laws solve the problem for the priest. No matter what a court may require, no matter what personal inconvenience or incarceration may result, unless he has the permission of the penitent the priest cannot reveal the contents of the confessional. To do so would violate divine, natural, and ecclesiastical law and subject him to permanent excommunication. So far as these writers can determine there is no modern-day case where a priest has deliberately violated the seal of confession. He has always preferred jail and fines to excommunication.

Pragmatism and the Psychiatrist. On the other hand, psychotherapists and mental health practitioners face the problem of confidential communications with patients from a pragmatic clinical viewpoint and with the strong protection of a very specific code of ethics. They must have the counselee's complete confidence if they are to help the client. While many physical ailments can be treated with some degree of effectiveness by a doctor whom the patient does not trust completely, a psychiatrist or psychologist must work in an atmosphere of complete acceptance in which no secret feeling or act can be hidden. This is essential for the patient's recovery of emotional health. As Guttmacher and Weihofen express it:

The psychiatric patient confides more utterly than anyone else in the world. He exposes to the therapist not only what his words directly express; he lays bare his entire self, his dreams, his fantasies, his sins and his shame. Most patients who undergo psychotherapy know that this is what will be expected of them, and that they cannot get help except on that condition. . . . It would be too much to expect them to do so if they knew that all they say—and all that the psychiatrist learns from what they say—may be revealed to the world from a witness stand.[6]

In addition, the major professional associations of psychotherapists have developed professional codes of conduct that accredited practitioners commit themselves to. Deliberate violations of the code can result in sanctions against offending members of the profession.

The effect of these two factors is to solve the problem of whether to reveal confidences for most members of these professions. They may decide to do so, but if they do they know that they are damaging not only their own status as members of the profession but also the effectiveness of the entire profession. From a purely pragmatic standpoint, psychotherapists had best keep their professional secrets, even at risk of inconveniences and potential fines or jail sentences.

Of course, many states have recognized the physician-patient privilege. Increasingly, other psychotherapists and mental health practitioners are also securing protection by law so that their confidential communications are protected. But even where they are not, professional ethics demand that the therapist not reveal knowledge gained through a counseling interview. A number of members of the profession have paid fines and spent time in jail to defend this ethical and legal principle.

The Uneasy Status of the Minister and Rabbi. The Protestant minister of the gospel and the Jewish rabbi relate to this problem in yet a third way. For the most part, confession of sin is not a sacrament in their religious communities. Except for the Anglo-Catholic wing of the Episcopal Church, there is not an obligation to make confession for any member of a Protestant church or a Jewish temple or synagogue. Still, the oral confession of wrong to a trusted minister or rabbi, shared prayer seeking forgiveness or spiritual direction, the assurance of God's pardon or grace given on the authority of Christ's words or holy scripture, the experience of guilt or confusion removed and the emergence of new hope or insight—all are elements formally or informally present in an experience of pastoral or rabbinical counseling which make the act sacred in nature. The healing of souls happens through more than just natural integration of personality or insight into subconscious motivations. God is at work and present in this relationship and the pastoral work has brought wholeness to spirit, religious insight, and a promise of newness.

There must be a genuine trust between the clergy and congregant or their relationship cannot proceed to the deep level of understanding necessary for good pastoral care. While the average pastor or rabbi is not prepared to engage in depth therapy, there can be no hindrance to the counseling relationship which might cause those who seek help to hold back mention of the very act, feeling, or circumstance causing the most spiritual turmoil. Confidence must be complete if pastoral counseling is to be helpful. There must be no possibility of a disclosure of the shared confidences should a court of law call the pastor or rabbi as a witness.

Yet, what is the clergy to do if this eventuality occurs? There is no canon or doctrine in most Protestant denominations or in Judaism that forbids disclosure of confidences. Neither set of religious communities has worked out any statement which, for all, defines officially the pastoral or rabbinical counseling relationship. Most do not have any set or code of vocational or professional ethics such as those that bind psychotherapists.

This set of circumstances places the pastor and rabbi in a unique category before the law of the state. Able to rely neither on canon law nor on a specific professional code of ethics, their only ground for seeking immunity from disclosing pastoral confidences is the sovereign will of God at work in their calling, which can be neither proven nor bound, but which holds the clergy mightily within its grasp. The minister believes with heart and soul that the pastoral relationship is sacred and its confidences should be cherished as surely as that tie which binds husband and wife. Yet, since the relationship is not embedded in the doctrinal standards of the religious tradition or given the professional status of a psychiatrist's relationship with a patient, its standing before the state is more often analogous to that of a common-law marriage than to one properly solemnized by benefit of clergy. Sometimes recognized, often not, its existence seems an embarrassment to the courts where statutes give no recognition or inadequate standing to its recognition and protection.

The Scope of This Study. It is the purpose of this book to discover the status and prospects for what the law calls the priest-penitent privilege. There have been significant changes in the status of things since the original edition of this book appeared almost twenty years ago. Significant cases and court decisions will be reviewed and interpreted as they have helped shape some of the changes that have occurred in these two decades. We will look at the history of the seal of confession as it has come down to us from English common law and examine how it has fared under common and statute law. We will consider how the privilege affects clergy in the congregational setting and in newer forms of specialized ministries, as well as its contribution to raising some serious ethical questions for clergy. Finally, we will look at some unresolved issues still needing attention and offer some advice to clergy faced with making the hard decision of when and when not to reveal pastoral confidences.

The book is not exhaustive, nor (we hope) exhausting. Much relevant material has been omitted. Any reader interested in further study of specific points will find guidance in the references and notes cited for each chapter. We have attempted to sketch the framework of the issues involved. If the reader is helped by our investigation and the problems defined and clarified here, the writers will be pleased and gratified.

Chapter II / WHERE THE CLERGY AND THE LAW MEET

Most ministers, priests, and rabbis care little and know less about "the law." Capitalize the word, set it in the context of the Old Testament, and they may become experts. But ask them the difference between statute and common law, or question them about the legal rights of a minister under the rules of evidence and they fall silent. They may have brushed against the law briefly while paying a traffic ticket, and they may have read something by Erle Stanley Gardner, openly or surreptitiously depending on the cover, but these experiences have not prepared them for those times when they may need to know by what right they may speak or keep silence in a court of law.

Typical Cases. Perhaps one place we can begin our inquiry is to examine the kinds of cases that arise where the clergy and the law meet. We have already seen an example of what may happen in the painful experience of Ron Salfen, the Texas pastor who was sent to jail by a Texas judge. While matters do not usually progress to such lengths, Salfen's experience was not unique.

In 1968, the Reverend J. R. White, pastor of First Baptist Church in Montgomery, Alabama, was called as a witness in a divorce proceeding involving a couple who were members of his congregation and with whom he had counseled. When he was questioned about matters one of the parties to the divorce action had discussed with him, he declined to answer, claiming the protection of Alabama's traditional privilege communication law. The judge ruled that, since there is no discipline in the Baptist Church that enjoins confession or compels members to seek the advice of clergy, the statute did not apply to Dr. White. He was compelled to testify.[1]

Danny Wainscott was arrested and charged with the murder of a young woman in Franklin County, Kentucky, in 1978. While in jail, Danny asked that this friend, the Reverend Larry Weiss, be called and given permission to visit him at the Franklin County jail. During the visit, the man confessed that he had committed the murder and asked the pastor to relay the information to the police. The pastor did. At the trial, Mr. Weiss was called as a witness and told the court of his conversation with Danny. The defense raised no objection to the testimony by the minister. Wainscott was convicted and sentenced to life in prison. On appeal, the defense raised a question of the privilege regarding the minister's testimony and alleged that the trial court had acted improperly in permitting the testimony. The higher court rejected the argument on the grounds that Wainscott had given Weiss information with the request that it be given to a third party not present. Therefore, Kentucky's new privilege statute would not apply in this situation.[2] But some felt it should have. And should the minister have allowed himself to be used as a go-between this way?

One of the best-known cases is that of Dr. Emil Swenson, a Lutheran pastor in Minneapolis who had counseled with the husband in a family conflict which finally led to divorce. When the case came to trial, the wife had Pastor Swenson subpoenaed to testify in her favor and against her husband.

The pastor appeared, but declined to answer certain questions regarding matters discussed with him by the husband. He was held in contempt of court. On appeal, Swenson was cleared of the contempt charge and his case has become a highly celebrated one in the annals of clergy-penitent litigation.[3] Among the findings in the court's opinion:

> It is a matter of common knowledge and we take judicial notice of the fact, that such "discipline" is traditionally enjoined upon all clergymen by the practice of their respective churches. Under such "discipline" enjoined by such practice all faithful clergymen render such help to the spiritually sick and cheerfully offer consolation to supplicants who come in response to the call of conscience.

Not all courts have been so generous. In a 1965 California case[4] a rabbi, who had counseled both parties in a situation that ended in a divorce action, was called as a witness. The court held that the statute did not apply to communication made to one of the clergy acting as a marriage counselor, because the statute specifically covered only confessions made in the ordinary course of discipline enjoined by the church. The opinion stated:

> It would wrench the language of the statute to hold that it applies to communications made to a religious or spiritual advisor acting as a marriage counselor. We think this result regrettable for reasons of public policy . . . but the wording of the statute leaves us no choice.

In a 1961 Pennsylvania case a Catholic priest was required to testify in a case involving a will contest. The priest visited a woman in her home prior to her death to receive a gift. While he was there, the woman told him that she had no will. The court held that while the communication came "in the course of the priest's duties," it was not made in confidence to a spiritual advisor, and that the woman was neither seeking nor receiving spiritual advice or absolution. Thus, the communication was not privileged.[5]

Mikco Steven Ball was charged with murder in Indiana in 1981. On January 3, a Saturday, Ball telephoned the Reverend Purvis E. Lawson whose church Ball had attended for several months prior to his arrest. Ball requested an appointment with the pastor following the services the next day. At that time, Ball confessed to Lawson that he had killed three people. The pastor did not believe this at first, but encouraged Ball to turn himself in to the police, and Ball agreed to consider this possibility. The next day when the pastor told a police officer about the conversation, the officer told the pastor about three unsolved murders. That night, the pastor talked again with Ball and convinced him to surrender to the Indianapolis police.

During the trial Mr. Lawson was called as a witness for the prosecution and he testified freely and willingly. As a part of his testimony, Lawson said that he was pastor of Southside Baptist Church in Indianapolis and that he was not a graduate of any theological school. Lawson told the court that pastoral confession does not constitute one of the tenets of his church and that no discipline of the church would cause him to recognize a confidential pastor-parishioner relationship with respect to evidence of a crime. Further, he said, the fact that he was a minister would not affect his personal decision to testify. In light of these factors, the appeals court held that it was proper for the court to receive testimony from Mr. Lawson concerning anything told to him by Mikco Steven Ball. Indiana's privileged communications statute would not be applicable to this case.[6] But should it have been?

Divorce actions, paternity suits, child custody cases, child abuse charges, estate settlements and will contests, murder trials and rape cases: these are some of the kinds of cases for which clergy have been sought as witnesses and asked to tell in court of conversations they have had in confidence. In most cases the result has been satisfactory to the clergy, but not always. Consider the case of the unfortunate Mr. Williams.[7]

The Reverend Frank Williams was pastor of Mt. Zion Baptist Church in Greensboro, N. C. He refused to take the oath or to testify in the trial of a criminal action involving the rape of a young girl, on the grounds that all parties were members of his church and he had held pastoral conversations with all of them. He said he "did not want to take sides." In pressing Williams to be sworn and to answer some general questions, Judge Walter E. Brock made clear that he would respect the confidentiality of specific privileged conversations. Williams refused even to be sworn. Judge Brock held him in contempt and sentenced him to ten days in jail.

Williams appealed the contempt citation, contending that he possessed information that he had received in confidence, in his role as a minister of the gospel. To be forced to testify would violate his rights under the First and Fourteenth Amendments to the U. S. Constitution, he claimed. His appeal was denied by the North Carolina Supreme Court, which concluded that the minister's refusal to be sworn was "willful, deliberate, unlawful and punishable summarily." The court said:

> The fact that one called as a witness fears that his testimony may decrease the esteem in which he is held in the community, or may decrease his ability to render service therein, does not justify refusal by him to testify in response to questions otherwise proper. . . . It is the right to exercise one's religion or lack of it which is protected, not one's sense of ethics.

What is clear in the cases cited is that neither the minister nor the courts have understood with sufficient clarity the rights and responsibilities of clergy in matters of privileged communications. In the next chapter we will begin to trace the history of this misunderstanding.

Chapter III / HOW IT ALL BEGAN

The pastor's instinct to silence about confidential communications is not based on current whim. The roots of this privilege go back to the time of the church fathers. Wrapped up with the church's practice of auricular confession, the privilege developed over a period of several hundred years. In this chapter we shall trace briefly its history as it developed in the faith and practice of the Holy Catholic Church.

The Bible. The Bible records several examples of the confession of sins. Generally, these are public confessions. In the New Testament there is the record of those who came to the River Jordan to John the Baptist, and who "were baptized of him . . . confessing their sins" (Matthew 3:6; Mark 1:5 KJV). In the Acts of the Apostles we find that in Ephesus "many that believed came, and confessed, and shewed their deeds," either to the apostle Paul or to the church (Acts 19:18).[1] James, in that section of his letter that has to do with faith and healing, exhorts his readers to "confess your sins to one another, and pray for one another, that you may be healed" (James 5:16). But no one is sure of the extent of confession as a general practice of the church before the end of the first century.

The Church Fathers. The origin of the seal (secrecy) of confession in the apostolic church is also obscure. The early church father Clement I (died A.D. 99), exhorted the Corinthians: "You therefore who laid the foundation of the disorder must submit to the elders and be disciplined so as to repent, bending the knees of your hearts" (I Clement 57:1).[2] But no mention is made of the absolutely confidential nature of a confession until sometime later. Tertullian, who died in 225, insisted that the knowledge of sins a person may have committed be confined to the congregation.[3] This was during the period when church members were obligated to confess their sins before the whole congregation and do open penance. Paulinus in his *Life of St. Ambrose* (d. 397) says that Ambrose wept with penitents when they came to him for confession and that he "never revealed to any but the Lord" what had been divulged to him.[4] Others in this same period who practiced the secrecy of confessed material were the Syrian church father Aphreates, Abraham of Kidun, and Asterius of Amasea.[5] A little later, St. Augustine (d. 430) in his writings, especially *Sermo 82,* "repeatedly emphasizes that he endeavors to heal secret sins in secret, without exposing them. . . ."[6]

Papal Recognition. The first papal recognition of the secrecy of the confessional was by Leo I (bishop of Rome from 440 to 461). In a letter to the bishops at Campania, Samnium, and Picenum, he wrote that the manifestation of conscience in secret confession to the priests fully sufficed and had for a long time been customary in the church. Public confession of sins was not necessary and was, in fact, to be stopped. Where confessors were betraying the secrecy of the confessional, he wrote:

> I prescribe that that presumption *contrary to the apostolic rule,* which I have lately learned is being committed by certain illicit

usurpers, be utterly banished. Clearly, concerning the penitence which is demanded by the faithful, one must not read publicly the notes of a written confession on the nature of each individual sin, since it suffices that the state of conscience be indicated *in secret confession* to the priests alone. Although one must praise that plenitude of faith which, through fear of God, does not shrink from blushing before men, yet since the sins of all those who seek penance are not of such a nature that they do not fear to have them published abroad, it is necessary to desist from this custom, of which one cannot approve, lest many be put off from availing themselves of the remedies of penance, either through shame or through fear of seeing revealed to their enemies deeds for which they may be subject to the action of the law. Moreover, that confession is sufficient which is made firstly to God, and then also to the priest, who prays for the sins of the penitents. Only then will many allow themselves to be summoned to penance, if the conscience of him who is confessing is not to be revealed to the ears of the people.[7]

Here we have, as Kurtscheid states, the first pope "who plainly and unequivocally demands only secret confession and strict silence on the part of the confessor."[8]

In the Eastern Church, we also find an early recognition of the seal. A decree of the Second Synod of Dwin (554) in Armenia, the twentieth canon, reads: "A priest who reveals the confession of the penitents shall be deposed with anathema." Other passages from this same decree give sufficient information for us to judge the importance attached to the inviolability of the confessional by this branch of the Holy Catholic Church.[9]

But in the Western Church, during the period after Leo I, there is no documentary evidence concerning the seal until the ninth century, neither in the decrees of the councils nor in the penitential books in use during this period.[10] Then, in 802, Paulinus of Aquileia observed that a priest "like a wise and perfect physician should know how to heal and cleanse wounds and not to talk about them."[11] Evidently, medical

ethics as found particularly in the Hippocratic Oath may
have offered a helpful example to the clergy at this point.

About the middle of the ninth century, Frankish councils
introduced limited measures of the sort necessary to ensure
the secrecy of the confessional in that realm. And sometime
later, Burchard of Worms, in a manual written about
1008-12, "sternly warns that a priest so offending is to be
deposed and made to do penance in perpetual pilgrimage,
deprived of all honor." The Old Irish *Speckled Book*, which,
though formulated late, reflects early usage, "makes the
divulgence of a confession one of the four offenses so grave
that for them no penance is possible."[12]

Papal Legislation. At the close of the ninth century there is
the first *direct* penal legislation of the Western church
against the violation of the seal. In the *Poenitentiale
Summorum Pontificum,* canon 105, a double punishment is
inflicted on a priest who violates the seal: he is to be removed
from office and he is to go into lifelong exile.[13]

As time went on and the institution of the confession
became established in church practice, more specific
legislative references to its secret nature are found. In the
"Decretum" of the Gratian who compiled the edicts of
previous councils and the principles of church law,
published about 1151, there is a restatement of the
declaration of the law as to the seal of the confessional: "Let
the priest who dares to make known the sins of his penitent
be deposed." Further, the violator of this law was to be made
a lifelong, ignominious wanderer.[14] Canon 21 of the Fourth
Lateran Council (1215), binding on the whole church, again
lays down the obligation to secrecy:

Let the priest absolutely beware that he does not by word or
sign or by any manner whatever in any way betray the sinner:
but if he should happen to need wiser counsel let him

cautiously seek the same without any mention of person. For whoever shall dare to reveal a sin disclosed to him in the tribunal of penance we decree that he shall be not only deposed from the priestly office but that he shall also be sent into the confinement of a monastery to do perpetual penance.[15]

Notice here that neither this canon nor the "Decretum" implies that the necessity for secrecy in the confessional is a new teaching of the church.

Current Practice. Since the fifteenth century, canonists and theologians have been unanimous in emphasizing the strict obligation of the seal of confession. Reaffirmed many times, the seal stands as secure today in the Roman Catholic Church as it did during the late Middle Ages. Whether or not it has been granted legal recognition, the seal binds the lips of every priest. The Catholic who comes to confession can be assured that his words will never be repeated.

Post-Vatican II Developments. Since the Second Vatican Council, two new documents have underscored the continuing sanctity of confession. Just prior to Lent 1976 the revised rite of the Sacrament of Penance was introduced in the United States. The Latin text for the rite was promulgated by Pope Paul VI on December 2, 1973, and its translation and worldwide use was left to the national bishops.

The new rite was widely misinterpreted, however. Some concluded before the English language rite was published that the reforms of Vatican II had made confession unnecessary. A general decline in the number and a substantial change in the nature of penitential confessions has been noted and documented in many press reports. In fact, in April 1974 the Holy Father found it necessary to reaffirm the meaning of the decree on this sacrament and to add quite pointedly that the traditional confessional must be retained.[16]

The seal of the confessional is provided for in the text of the new rite and the introduction to it: "As the minister of God the confessor comes to know the secrets of another's conscience, and he is bound to keep the sacramental seal of confession absolutely inviolate."[17]

As 1982 was coming to an end, the new text for a major revision of canon law was promulgated in the United States. In several of its sections the document now deals with the question at hand:

> Can. 937-1. The sacramental seal is inviolable. For that reason the confessor is bound by obligation not to betray in any measure the penitent for any cause whatsoever, either by word or in any other manner.
>
> -2. An interpreter, if one was employed, and all other persons who have in any way come to a knowledge of sins from a confession are also bound by obligation to observe secrecy.
>
> Can. 938-1. The confessor is totally forbidden to use the knowledge acquired from confession to the detriment of the penitent even when any danger whatsoever of revelation is excluded.
>
> Can. 1340-1. A confessor who directly violates the seal of confession incurs an automatic *(latae sententiae)* excommunication. If he does so only indirectly, he should be punished in accord with the seriousness of the offense.
>
> -2. An interpreter or other persons mentioned in canon 937-2 who violate this secrecy should be punished with a just penalty, not excluding excommunication.

Chapter IV / THE COMMON LAW CAME OUT OF ENGLAND

The common law of England had its origin in the ancient rules and customs of the people. During these times there was a very close connection between the church and the state. It is not surprising, then, that we find the seal of confession recognized in early English common law, even though this recognition no longer applied at the time of the Revolution, when America fixed her heritage of English common law.

Anglo-Saxon England. In Anglo-Saxon England, prior to the Norman Conquest, early legal codes provide us with a recognition of the confessional as such, although, except in one instance, no mention is made regarding its seal. The Anglo-Saxon laws of Edward the Elder (921-24), son of Alfred the Great, state: "And if a man guilty of death (i.e., who has incurred the penalty of death) desires confession let it never be denied him."[1] This same law is found repeated in the forty-fourth of the secular laws of King Canute (1017-35).[2] Just prior to Canute's reign, in the laws of King Ethelred who ruled England from 978 to 1016, we find this provision: "And let every Christian man do as is needful to him: let him strictly keep his Christianity and accustom

39

himself frequently to shrift (i.e., confess): and fearlessly declare his sins."[3]

The existence at this early date of secrecy about confessed matters can be inferred. A Catholic writer makes the inference.

> The very close connexion between the religion of the Anglo-Saxons and their laws, many of which are purely ordinances of religious observance enacted by the State, the repeated recognition of the supreme jurisdiction of the pope, and the various instances of the application in the Church of England of the laws of the Church in general lead conclusively to the opinion that the ecclesiastical law of the secrecy of confession was recognized by the law of the land in Anglo-Saxon England.[4]

This inference seems justified. In fact, there is some reason to support the contention that in Anglo-Saxon England prior to the Norman Conquest the seal of confession was absolute, without any exceptions, even the one later recognized where the priest was required to divulge information obtained during the confessional if it was of a treasonous character. Mr. Justice W. F. Finlason, in a footnote to the case of Regina v. Hay (1860), remarks that in Best on Presumptive Evidence,

> . . . The learned writer, in support of the exception [for treason] suggests, cited from the "Ancient Laws and Institutes of England," a passage from the "Laws of Henry I"; a comparison of which with the Saxon law in the same work (to which Lord Coke alludes as the sources of our common law) will show that the recognition [of the seal of confession] was of Saxon, and the exception of Norman origin. The sanctity of confession, with that exception, has been recognized [under English common law].[5]

This observation appears to be extremely significant. Not only does it refer to an ancient Saxon law that recognizes the seal of confession, but it also points out that when the seal was originally recognized no exceptions were allowed.

Post-Norman England. Between the time of the Norman Conquest in 1066 and the Reformation, the English councils were not reluctant to enjoin the law of the church concerning the inviolability of the seal of confession. In the old laws of Henry I (1100-1135), a Norman and the second son of William the Conqueror, we find this passage (Leges Hen. I., c. 5, § 17): "Priests should guard that they not reveal to acquaintances or strangers what has been confessed to them by those who come for confession; for if they do it, even in good faith, they will be sentenced to live all the days of their life as an honorless pilgrim."[6] And in 1220, the Council of Durham declared:

> A priest shall not reveal a confession—let none dare from anger or hatred or fear of the Church or of death, in any way to reveal confessions, by sign or word, general or special, as (for instance), by saying, "I know what manner of men ye are," under peril of his Order and Benefice, and if he shall be convicted thereof he shall be degraded without mercy.[7]

A similar canon is found in the actions of the provincial Council of Oxford, held in 1222, in which degradation is prescribed for any breach of the seal. The same law is also found in the 21st canon of the Lateran Council, which was declared in the Acts of the Synod of Exeter in 1287.

Again in this period after the Norman Conquest we have good grounds for inferring that the secular courts recognized the seal. The Roman Catholic Church was the church of the nation, and church laws were emphatic on the subject. But this recognition would not have rested on any principle of immunity from disclosure of confidential communications made to clergy. It would have rested on the fact that confession was a sacrament, that the doctrine of the church laid it down as a necessity, that both king and people practiced it in some degree of faithfulness, and that the practice was wholly a matter of spiritual discipline on which the church had declared the law of absolute secrecy. In their joint *History of English Law,* Sir Frederick Pollock and Professor Maitland support this position. They say that the *jus commune* or common law of the universal church was the law of the Church in England.[8]

Lyndwood—The English Canonist. Important material on the history of the seal of the confession during this period is contained in the "Provinciale" of Lyndwood (Oxford, 1679), the only great English canonist. This "Provinciale" consists of the provincial constitutions of fourteen arch-bishops of Canterbury from Stephen Langton (d. 1228) to Henry Chichele (d. 1443). In it is a constitution of Walter, Archbishop of Canterbury, apparently Walter Reynolds, transferred from the See of Worcester to the primatial see in 1313. As a part of it are these words:

> Also let no priest dare from anger, hatred or fear, even of death, to disclose in any manner whatsoever, whether by sign, gesture or word, in general or in particular, anybody's confession. And if he shall be convicted of this he shall be, deservedly, degraded, without hope of reconciliation.[9]

Later, Lyndwood deals with a priest's being found guilty of revealing a confession. He says: "But what if the person confessing consents to its being revealed, because, per-chance, he calls the Confessor as a witness?" His answer is:

> The doctors say that he may reveal it. But understand this in such way that the priest shall on no account reveal that which he knows only through confession. . . . But the person who has confessed can intimate the matter to him in some other way which gives him leave to reveal it: and then he can tell, but,

none the less, he ought to avoid scandal as much as possible. For he is bound to conceal the confession for two reasons, viz., on account of the sacrament, because it is almost of the essence of the sacrament to conceal the confession . . . : likewise for reason of the scandal. The first is removed by the permission of the person confessing, but the second remains none the less: and, therefore, where scandal is to be feared, he ought not to make use of such permission.

Lyndwood is willing to consider some of the problems that go along with any discussion of the seal of confession. One of these is whether the pledge of silence applies to the confession of a sin to be committed in the future. He writes:

But I ask—what if confession is made of some sin about to be committed, but not yet committed? For instance, some one confesses that he wants to kill a man or to commit some other misdeed and he says that he is unable to resist the temptation. May the priest reveal it? Some say that he may reveal it to such a person as can be beneficial and not detrimental . . . , but the doctors of theology in this case say in general . . . that he must not reveal it, but must keep it entirely secret. . . . Henry de Segusio says, however, that whatever he can properly . . . do for the prevention of the sin, he ought to do, but without mention of person and without betrayal of him who makes the confession. Others say that where the confession is one of a sin about to be committed it is not a real confession, and that to the person making it, a penance cannot be given . . . and for these reasons it may be revealed to those who can be beneficial and not detrimental as I have said before [quoting Rudovicus and Guido of Baysio].[10]

Lyndwood also considers what a priest should do if a judge presses him too hard on the contents of a confession.

One may deduce from the premises that if a judge maliciously presses and inquires of a priest whether he knows anything of such a fact, which he has, perhaps, heard in confession, if he cannot, by changing the subject or by some other means, turn aside the unjust judge, he can answer that he knows nothing thenceforth . . . , because it is secretly understood . . . "as man"; or he can say simply "I know nothing through confession" because it is secretly understood "nothing to be revealed to you."[11]

These statements of Lyndwood and his citation of various authorities give us strong indication of the law of English ecclesiastical courts before the Reformation. Historical records establish that the King's Court in ancient days was manned by bishops and leading clerics, so that canon and common law were inextricably involved with each other in the determination of cases before such courts. Pollock and Maitland's *History of English Law* tells us that on the 16th of July, 1195, there sat in the Court of King's Bench an archbishop, three bishops, and three archdeacons. It further states that

> . . . it is by popish clergymen that our English common law is converted from a rude mass of customs into an articulate system, and when the "popish clergymen" yielding at length to the pope's commands no longer sit as the principal justices of the king's court the golden age of the common law is over.[12]

It is highly improbable that at a period when systematization of the common law was being handled by "popish clergymen" a rule compelling the disclosure of confession would have grown up. Furthermore, there is not a single reported case, textbook or commentary, during the whole pre-Reformation period which contains any suggestion that the laws of evidence did not respect the seal of confession. These grounds seem sufficient to lead to the conclusion that before the Reformation the seal was regarded as sacred by the common law of England.[13]

Articuli Cleri—A Misunderstood Statute. The only recorded statute of the English Parliament which deals with the right of confession is Statute I of the ninth year of Edward II. Known as *Articuli Cleri,* it was enacted in 1315. The most accurate version is found in Best and is taken from the valuable work entitled: *Statutes of the Realm, printed by command of his Majesty, King George the Third, in pursuance of an Address of the House of Commons: From Original Records and Authentic Manuscripts.* The work is dated 1810. We will notice later that it differs from the version given by Sir Edward Coke in the *2nd Institute.* Translated, the significant part of the statute reads: "And the King's pleasure is that thieves or appellors (whensoever they will) may confess their offences to priests, but let the confessors beware that they do not erroneously inform such appellors."[14]

In later years, after the Reformation and at the time of the persecution of Roman churchmen, Sir Edward Coke, then Attorney General, referred to this statute to establish the privilege of the confession, but added that it did not apply in the case of treason. In the *2nd Institute,* page 629, he expresses himself as follows:

Latrones vel appellatores [evildoers and/or prosecuted ones]. This branch extendeth only to thieves and approvers indicted of felony, but extendeth not to high treasons: for if high treason be discovered to the confessor, he ought to discover it, for the danger that thereupon dependeth to the king and the whole realm, therefore this branch declareth the common law, that the privilege of confession extendeth only to felonies: And albeit, if a man indicted of felony becometh an approver, he is sworn to discover all felonies and treasons, yet he is not in degree of an approver in law, but only of the offense whereof he is indicted; and for the rest, it is for the benefit of the king, to move him to mercy: So as this branch beginneth with thieves, extendeth only to approvers of thievery or felony, and not to appeals of treason; for by the common law, a man indicted of high treason could not have the benefit of clergy (as it was holden in the king's time, when this act was made), nor any clergyman privilege of confession to conceal high treason: and so was it resolved in 7 Hen[ry] V. (Rot. Parl. anno

7 Hen[ry] V.nu. 13) whereupon Friar John Randolph, the Queen Dowager's confessor, accused her of treason, for compassing of the death of the king: And so was it resolved in the case of Henry Garnet (Hil. 3 Jac.), superior of the Jesuits in England, who would have shadowed his treason under the privilege of confession, &c.; and albeit this act extendeth to felonies only, as hath been said, yet the caveat given to the confessors is observable, ne erronice informent [they should not erroneously give information].[15]

Best says that he cites this passage to show the common law on the subject but that it is very doubtful whether the caveat at the end of the above enactment was inserted to warn the confessor against disclosing the secrets of the penitent to others. Rather, the grammatical construction and context seem to show that it was to prevent the confessor from abusing his privilege of access to the criminal by conveying information to him from without. The clause is translated this way in the best editions of the statutes, such as the edition used by Best and the edition of Ruffhead in 1762.[16]

Because of Lord Coke's gloss on this statute its essential meaning was obscured for many later jurists, and it is still referred to occasionally by contemporary commentators as a proof of the fact that the seal of confession, with the exception for treason, was recognized by English parliamentary law. But this is simply counter to the plain meaning of the statute. In essence, what we find here is an early recognition by English law that certain prisoners had the right to be confessed by a priest, but that the priest should not take advantage of the situation by conveying to the prisoner undesirable information from the outside.

On the other hand, this statement of Lord Coke's is interesting because it shows his respect for the rule of the secrecy of the confessional by the emphasis he puts on the exception. Evidently, the privilege of confession was not at that time restricted to Anglican priests, but was allowed to

Roman Catholic ones as well. Lord Coke is citing what he feels to be the common law at that time, as it would apply to all priests. By supporting his statement with reference to the then recent Guy Fawkes case and the Gunpowder Plot, in which Henry Garnet was involved, along with his own argument, we have strong evidence that this great common lawyer was of the opinion that even in his post-Reformation period the common law of England recognized the privilege of confession, except in the case of treason. Coming from so distinguished a lawyer and fierce champion of Protestantism, this is a most significant viewpoint.[17]

In conclusion we can say that once recognized by the church, practice of the seal of confession spread quickly, so that we find it upheld in England before the Norman Conquest in 1066. There is good evidence to conclude that the seal was absolute in these Anglo-Saxon times and that the exception for treason did not arise until after the Norman invasion. Even during these early years, the penalty for violation of the seal by a priest was very stringent, usually involving deposition from his charge and the necessity to do penance for life.

Because the religion of the Anglo-Saxons was closely tied in with their laws, there is also good reason to believe that the seal of confession was recognized as the law of the land in pre-Norman England. This recognition continued throughout Norman times during the period of the formation of English common law. During those years Roman Catholic ecclesiastical officials sat as judges in the King's Court. The recognition of the seal continued up to the time of the Reformation and beyond. However, the often-referred-to English statute, *Articuli Cleri,* does not guarantee the right of the secrecy of the confession but only affirms the right of prisoners to receive confession. So far as can be determined there is no pre-Reformation *parliamentary* law which recognizes the seal.

Chapter V / ANGLICANS
AND THE RIGHT
TO SILENCE

Post-Reformation England. After the Reformation in England, the privilege attached to the confessional continued, at least for a time, as in pre-Reformation days. There was no statute to take it away and, on the contrary, the First Book of Common Prayer in 1549 contained services, such as the Ordination Service and the Visitation of the Sick, in which the clergy received power to give absolution and were expressly directed in certain cases to administer it. The cases in which they were so directed were just those in which alone it had been obligatory, as members of the Roman Catholic Church, to confess (i.e., weighty and grievous sins). And the form of the absolution (*ego te absolvo,* etc.) was precisely that used by Roman Catholic priests; it was judicial or sacramental and not merely declaratory as in the Morning and Evening Services.[1] This meant, in essence, that if the form and meaning of confession did not change, neither did the privileged relationship between penitent and priest, so long as there was no law to the contrary.

In addition, the Communion Office of the Anglican Church contained these words which, by implication, recognized the seal:

And if there be any of you whose conscience is troubled or grieved in anything, lacking comfort or counsel, let him come to me, or to some other discreet and learned priest, taught in the law of God, and confess and open his grief *secretly* [italics mine], that he may receive such ghostly counsel, advice and comfort, that his conscience may be relieved, and that of us (as of the ministers of God and of the Church) he may receive comfort and absolution, to the satisfaction of his mind, and avoiding of all scruple or doubtfulness.[2]

Confession was, as we can see, now voluntary and not compulsory, but the provision was there that if the penitent came for private confession, he came under the protection of privileged communication.

Evaluating the implications of this, W. M. Best writes:

It follows, then, that not only was there nothing in the change which took place at the Reformation to alter the case as to the privilege attaching to confession, but that there was, on the contrary, an express recognition of it by statute. For of course the recognition of confession implies, in the absence of anything to the contrary, the recognition of its secrecy, because such was the common law rule; and if it were otherwise, no one would be likely to confess, and therefore the directions to the Anglican clergy, to exhort their penitents to confess, would be idle and futile.

. . . it is not so clear . . . that ministers of any other religious body, not believing in sacramental confession, would be entitled to it; at all events, according to the strict common law rule upon the subject, which, according to the clearest authority, applied only to sacramental confession with a view to sacramental absolution. But the later cases on the subject seem to extend the privilege to any communications made to a spiritual advisor as such, whether or not in sacramental confession.[3]

In the Second Prayer Book of 1552 the word "secretly" was omitted from the Communion Office. But this could hardly have meant that there was no obligation of secrecy;

rather, there was apparently present a desire to avoid the terms of the medieval system, and to rest upon the authority of Scripture alone.[4] Hence, the omission.

The Canons of 1603. Perhaps the only place where the seal of the confession was imposed as a duty by the Anglican Church was in the Canons of 1603. Among this set of ecclesiastical laws is Canon 113, which deals with the suppression of evil deeds by the reporting of them by those who administer each parish. This canon provides for the presentment to the Ordinary by parsons, vicars, or curates of the crimes and iniquities committed in the parish. However, it contains one significant reservation:

> Provided always that if any man confess his secret and hidden sins to the minister for the unburdening of his conscience, and to receive spiritual consolation and ease of mind from him; we do not in any way bind the said minister by this our Constitution, but do straitly charge and admonish him, that he do not at any time reveal and make known to any person whatsoever any crime or offense so committed to his trust and secrecy (except they be such crimes as by the laws of the realm his own life may be called in question for concealing the same), under pain of irregularity.[5]

The exception in this canon is enlightening. It would seem to imply that the English civil courts of this period recognized the inviolability of confession, except where the crime or planned action confessed was so serious that even a knowledge of it by others made them subject to capital punishment unless they revealed it. In such circumstances, a priest or pastor had no more privilege before the law than any other citizen.

A Roman Catholic writer is critical of this statute in the Anglican Canons of 1603. He says that the exemption is a marked departure from the pre-Reformation ecclesiastical law on the subject, and that, even apart from the exemption, the language used to declare the injunction bears a marked contrast to the language used to declare the secrecy in pre-Reformation days. This means, he says, that the Established Church of England did not claim for its confession the same absolute inviolability claimed by the Roman Catholic Church. He goes on to say:

> In view of the absolute repudiation by the State of the jurisdiction of the Catholic Church and in view of the abandonment of the Sacrament of Confession as practised before the Reformation, one may fairly presume that, from the date of that event, confession would no longer have been regarded as a ground, from motives of public policy, entitling to an exemption from the principle of the disclosure of all the truth known about the cause, were it to be civil or criminal.[6]

The writer is, of course, correct in his indictment of the Anglican Church for bowing before civil law by including the exemption. But he forgets that there is some evidence that English common law prior to the Reformation did not recognize the privilege in the case of treason. However, common law did recognize the seal of confession in all other cases and continued to do so for some years after the Reformation, when confession was still inviolable whether it was made to a Roman Catholic priest or to an Anglican one. This continued recognition of the privilege was based on motives of public policy.

Earlier and later writers and preachers of the church, such as Hugh Latimer, Thomas Bacon, Thomas Cranmer, Richard Hooker, George Herbert, William Laud, Jeremy Taylor, Edward Pusey, John Keble, and the American high churchman, James O. S. Huntington, all advocated confession as a necessary discipline of the Christian and defined the good confessor as a "discreet" person.[7] But there are no more absolute injunctions to secrecy except as this necessity may be implied from the nature of confession itself.

Privileges of Confession Withdrawn. From the point of view of the English civil courts, the privileges of the confessional were withdrawn from the English clergy sometime during the seventeenth century, perhaps with the banning of the prayer book of the Church of England. Wigmore concluded that after the restoration of the monarchy in 1660, with the return to the throne of Charles II, the English courts no longer recognized the seal.[8] Sir William Blackstone, who put out his monumental work on the common law about the time of the American Revolution, ignores completely the privilege of the confessional.[9]

No writer seems clear about the exact time the privilege was withdrawn, nor why. If, as seems most likely, the withdrawal occurred in January, 1645, with the abolition by Parliament of the Anglican Prayer Book, the reason would be that the substituted Directory for Worship just produced by the Westminster Assembly contained no provisions for private confession and absolution. These rites had been associated with the Episcopacy, abolished two years earlier. The Puritans had little patience with former Anglican ordinances. So, the seal of confession became meaningless when confession itself was abolished.

If Wigmore is right that the seal endured Puritan rule and was abolished after the Restoration, the reason would be quite different. With the return of Charles II, severe repressive measures were taken against the Puritan ministry, such as the Act of Uniformity of 1662, the First Conventicle Act of 1664, the "Five Mile Act" of 1665, and the Second Conventicle Act of 1670. The withdrawal of the seal would have been one more act of persecution, aimed at preventing the Puritan pastors from holding back secrets before royal tribunals, even though the Puritans did not practice confession as such. However, since we can only speculate about what actually happened, it seems more logical to conclude that the seal never endured Cromwell's "toleration."

There have been efforts to restore the privilege to confession in the Anglican Church, but they have not been successful. In a signed article to *The New York Times,* Kenneth Love writes from London:

> The Most Rev. Geoffrey Fisher, Archbishop of Canterbury, said today that the secrecy of confessions made to priests could not be sanctioned in the canon law of the Church of England until Parliament changed the laws of evidence.
>
> Addressing the convocation of Canterbury at Church House here, he urged reaffirmation of the principle of secrecy of the confessional. But he noted that priests had no statutory right to refuse to answer a judge in a court of law.
>
> Last year the convocation, seeking to avoid a clash with Parliament, deleted a clause from a draft canon dealing with secrecy of confession. The agenda of the present session of the convocation includes a resolution that would reaffirm the principle of secrecy without giving it legal protection and another stating that the church would welcome parliamentary action to exempt priests from the requirements governing court testimony.
>
> The Church of England is the state church and its canon law becomes the law of the land upon the assent of the sovereign, who is the head of the church as well as the chief of state. Royal assent, which is also required for acts of Parliament, would almost certainly be refused for canon laws to which Parliament objected. . . .
>
> The present canon governing secrecy of the confessional dates from 1603 and is regarded as largely obsolete. . . . A Church of England spokesman said the seal of confession had not been tested in the courts, at least in modern times, and that, in any case, an Anglican priest would probably go to jail rather than disclose a confession.[10]

Undoubtedly, efforts to restore the official recognition of the seal in the Anglican Church will be complicated so long as Parliament must approve all canon laws which the sovereign is asked to sign. But it is significant that the seal is informally subscribed to by Anglican priests today and that the statement would be made that they would probably go to jail rather than reveal the contents of a confession. By this attitude present-day Anglicanism holds to those traditions present in its life since Reformation times.

Current Practice in The Episcopal Church. The executive office of the General Convention of The Episcopal Church has issued a "memorandum on 'Privileged Communications' in The Episcopal Church." It states that there are no specific provisions in either the constitution or the canons of that denomination dealing with this subject. The constitution of the church provides, however, that the General Convention shall adopt "The Book of Common Prayer and Administration of the Sacraments and the Rites and Ceremonies of the Church" which "shall be in use in all the Dioceses."[11]

Included in each *Book of Common Prayer* adopted by the church have been rubrics which are complementary to the canons and which also carry the force of law in the church. In 1979, meeting in Denver, the General Convention adopted a new *Book of Common Prayer.* In that new prayer book is this rubric dealing with the "Rite of the Reconciliation of the Penitent": "The content of a confession is not normally a matter of subsequent discussion. The secrecy of a confession is morally absolute for the confessor and must under no circumstances be broken."[12]

This rubric carries the force of canon law and "molds the basis for discipline under the Canons of The Episcopal Church. Title IV. Canon 1 Sec. 1 provides as one of the offences for which a Bishop, Presbyter, or Deacon shall be liable to presentment to trial: '(3) Violation of the Rubrics of the Book of Common Prayer.'"[13]

According to this interpretation, "the absolute secrecy of any disclosures in the penitential relationship is ordered by The Episcopal Church." The Memorandum for the Presiding Bishop's Office concludes with this guarantee of the seal of confession:

> Notwithstanding any restraints, demands, or privileges imposed or conferred by civil law, the clergy of The Episcopal Church are bound to the secrecy of the confessional and the inviolate priest-penitent relationship. The obligation rises above the demands of the civil legal system.[14]

Chapter VI/LUTHER
REFORMS CONFESSION

When Martin Luther began his study and work toward the reformation of the church, one of the institutions which came under his scrutiny was the sacrament of penance. He admitted its desirability and, at first, recognized it as a legitimate sacrament of the church, although he hesitated later because of the lack of a divinely instituted sign. Eventually penance became for him "nothing but a return to baptism."[1] Confession under Luther and Lutheranism, however, took on a different appearance than it had possessed in Catholicism.

Luther's Doctrine of Confession. Luther did away with, first of all, the compulsory nature of confession. A person confessed only when moved to confession and not at the stated intervals prescribed by Roman Catholic doctrine. Furthermore, not all sins had to be confessed but only those which greatly troubled the conscience. Hidden sins did not have to be rooted out by a lengthy period of self-examination. Luther removed the old distinction between mortal and venial sins and doubted that it was even possible for a person to confess all mortal sins, since no one could know those hidden mortal sins of the heart. The most mortal of all sins he considered to be our inability to believe that we are hateful in the sight of God because of damnable and mortal sin.[2]

In his study of the church fathers, Luther concluded that the sins they absolved were not the ones then being absolved by the priests. He wrote: "For we read in Augustine, Cyprian, and the other Fathers that those things which are bound and loosed are not mortal sins, but criminal offenses, i.e., those acts of which men can be accused and convicted."[3]

This meant for Luther that the sins to be confessed were those things of which one could be accused, either by others or by one's own conscience. And by conscience, he meant a healthy one, not one seared and deformed by human traditions but one which knew the commandments of God and knew that much more could be left solely to the goodness of God than committed to our own diligence. All this, of course, led to his classic statement that

> Confession should be brief, and should be a confession chiefly of those things which cause pain at the time of confession, and, as they say, "move to confession." For the sacrament of confession was instituted for the quieting, not for the disturbing, of the conscience.[4]

Perhaps the most radical change Luther proposed was his insistence that confession could be made to any Christian, not just to the priest. This applied both to open and to hidden sins. Furthermore, the brother or sister could grant absolution to the penitent as surely as it had in the past been granted by the priest.

Luther and the Seal. These changes by Luther in the nature of confession had two implications for the meaning of its seal. First, those sins now confessed by a penitent very often would be only those for which he or she might legitimately be punished by the state, i.e., "criminal offenses . . . of which men can be accused and convicted." Second, the person hearing this confession might be any Christian brother or sister and not necessarily a pastor. What would be the meaning of the seal of confession under these new circumstances? Would it still apply within the Lutheran fellowships as it had under Roman Catholicism?

What few records we have of Luther's thought on this subject seem to indicate that he continued to take the seal seriously. He felt that a Christian ought not to reveal the contents of a confession in a court of law. In one place he says:

> Within the church's sphere of authority we deal in secret with the conscience and do not take its jurisdiction from the civil estate. Therefore people should leave us undisturbed in our sphere of authority and should not drag into their jurisdiction what we do in secret. I, too, have given secret advice, and because the matter was secret, the advice was justly given in this way. If the affair comes under the jurisdiction of civil authority later on, we know nothing of it. Nor shall they drag us into the case.[5]

At another time Luther was asked whether such secrecy should be preserved if a person confesses an irreparable crime, such as infanticide. Would not the confessor have to testify against the person in court? Luther replied:

> By no means! For one must distinguish between the authority of the church and the authority of the state. The woman did not confess to me but to Christ. But what Christ keeps secret I, too, must keep secret and simply deny that I have heard anything. If Christ has heard anything, He may Himself say so. But during the absolution I should privately say to the woman: You harlot, never do that again.[6]

These statements make it quite clear that Luther himself believed in the inviolability of the seal. We may assume that his associates and the later leaders of the Lutheran Church followed him in this teaching, lacking any evidence to the contrary.

Later Lutherans and the Right to Silence. Today, confession is still an article of faith in the Lutheran denominations. All subscribe to the Augsburg Confession, which has as its eleventh article: "Of confession, they teach, that Private Absolution ought to be retained in the churches, although in confession an enumeration of all sins is not necessary. For it is impossible, according to the Psalm: 'Who can understand his errors?'" (Psalm 19:12).[7]

Furthermore, Luther's teaching on the seal of confession is considered authoritative. Carl Ferdinand Wilhelm Walther, the principal founder of the Lutheran Church, Missouri Synod, in his *American Lutheran Pastoral Theology* (1872) warmly approved private confession and absolution and defended the seal of the confession.[8]

Two contemporary Lutheran statements uphold this same viewpoint. On the recommendation of its Board of Social Missions, the 1960 Biennial Convention of The United Lutheran Church in America (now The Lutheran Church in America) adopted the following proposition:

> In keeping with the historic discipline and practice of the Lutheran Church and to be true to a sacred trust inherent in the nature of the pastoral office, no minister of The United Lutheran Church in America shall divulge any confidential disclosure given to him in the course of his care of souls or otherwise in his professional capacity, except with the express permission of the person who has confided in him or in order to prevent the commission of a crime.[9]

The Church Council of The American Lutheran Church adopted a similar resolution that same year. Referred from the Joint Union Committee and recommended for adoption by the District Presidents' Committee, the document states that:

> WHEREAS it has long been recognized that a part of the ministry of pastors of the Lutheran church is to hear confessions, to counsel with persons, and to give advice, comfort, and guidance to those who seek it; and
> WHEREAS it is imperative that, in order for such ministry to be effective, all such communications made to the pastor should be kept in the strictest confidence and should be disclosed to no one without the specific consent of the person making the communication; and
> WHEREAS it is a part of the traditional discipline and practice of the Lutheran church that a pastor should hold inviolate all communications made to him in his capacity as a pastor; therefore,
> BE IT RESOLVED: (1) That the Church Council recognizes and reaffirms that a part of the ministry of a Lutheran pastor is to counsel with persons, to receive their confessions, and to give advice, comfort, and guidance to those who seek it; and
> (2) That the Church Council recognizes and reaffirms that it is a part of the traditional discipline and practice of the Lutheran church that the pastor hold inviolate and disclose to no one the confessions and communications made to him as a pastor without the specific consent of the person making the communication.[10]

Of course, neither of these statements has any legal status. But they do provide a basis on which a Lutheran pastor might claim the rights of privileged communication, particularly if the state in which he or she resides recognizes such claims by statute.

Recent Influences in American Lutheranism. The issue of confidentiality for Lutherans was raised quite dramatically in 1973 when the Reverend Paul Boe was threatened with extended incarceration for refusing to violate confidences in his testimony to a federal grand jury. Dr. Boe was executive director of the Division of Social Service of the American Lutheran Church. His case is treated extensively in chapter 14. The American Lutheran Church entered the case and invited many other churches and church agencies to join as *Amici Curiae.* The Eighth Circuit Court of Appeals set aside a contempt citation imposed by the U. S. District Court for the District of South Dakota, ruling that Boe had been denied due process.

At the time of Boe's experience, the resolution of the American Lutheran Church, quoted above, was the policy statement of that denomination. While it is a strong and unequivocal position statement, the Boe experience led the ALC to examine the issue of confidentiality more closely. The constitution of the denomination now contains this provision:

> One of the functions, exercised regularly by members of the Clergy Roster and occasionally by those lay persons elected as an officer or as a member of national or district staff of this Church, is to counsel with persons, to receive their confessions, and to give advice, comfort, and guidance to those who seek it. This Church recognizes and affirms that it is a part of the traditional discipline and practice of the Lutheran Church that such confessions and communications be held inviolate and disclosed to no one without the specific consent of the person making the confession.[11]

Note that the discipline of this church claims the privilege for certain laypersons who hold positions of responsibility as officers or staff persons. There is no legal basis for such a claim, but the recent experience of several churches indicates that this is one of the issues yet to be resolved satisfactorily. No doubt it will continue to be raised both in the churches and in the courts.

The constitution of the larger Lutheran Church in

America provides for a recognition of the sacred trust given to the pastoral office, but provides an exception when criminal activity may be involved in the confidential communication. It says:

> In keeping with historic discipline and practice of the Lutheran Church and to be true to a sacred trust inherent in the nature of the pastoral office, no minister of the Lutheran Church in America shall divulge any confidential disclosure received in the course of the care of souls or otherwise in a professional capacity, except with the express permission of the person who has given confidential information or in order to prevent the commission of a crime.

Chapter VII / CONFESSION IN THE REFORMED CHURCHES

Zwingli. The Swiss Reformers followed the Lutherans in their revision of confession. Zwingli, for instance, felt that since it is God who forgives, confession should be only to him, the wound being shown to the Physician. However, if God is not fully known nor his grace comprehended as it is offered in Christ, then the penitent is not forbidden to unburden his conscience to a wise counselor, a minister of the Word. He administers wine and oil (the sharpness of repentance and the sweetness of grace) into the soul's wound. Zwingli maintained that "auricular confession is nothing but a consultation, in which we receive, from him whom God has appointed . . . advice as to how we can secure peace of mind." He wrote: "Let us, therefore, confess frequently to the Lord, let us begin a new life frequently, and if there is anything not clear let us go frequently to a wise scholar who looks not at the pocket-book but at the conscience!"[1] Zwingli endorsed a limited kind of private confession, considerably modified from the practice of Roman Catholicism.

Bullinger. Henry Bullinger was Zwingli's successor at Zurich, and the author of the Second Helvetic Confession. He discussed repentance and confession in that document.

He believed that confession should be made either to God alone or in the general confession of the worship service. There was neither a need nor a warrant for auricular confession.[2] However, he did provide for private confession in certain instances.

> We have no objection if someone who is oppressed by the burden of his sins and by unsettling temptations wishes to obtain advice, instruction and consolation privately from a servant of the church or from another brother who is well-grounded in the Word of God.[3]

The word "privately" included in this statement would seem to imply a recognition of the seal of confession, at least in some instances.

Calvin. John Calvin treated the medieval system of confession in a manner closely similar to Luther's. Under the old system, Calvin asserted, consciences had been tortured by the doctrine of contrition and driven to either pretense or despair. He was sarcastic about the obligation of an annual secret confession to a priest. The early church had not heard of it. He cited Chrysostom with approval:

> Confess your sins, that you may obliterate them. If you are ashamed to tell any one what sins you have committed, confess them daily in your soul. I say not that you should confess them to your fellow-servant, who may reproach you; confess them to God, who cures them. Confess your sins on your bed, that there your conscience may daily recognize its crimes.[4]

But Calvin realized that if the heart was penitent, the person would also wish to confess before the church. Provision was made for two kinds of *public* confession—in ordinary public worship and when public calamity had called attention to a common guilt.[5]

In addition, Calvin said that Scripture authorized two kinds of *private* confession: to one another and to an injured neighbor. Commenting on James 5:16 (". . . confess your sins to one another . . ."), he wrote:

> Therefore, let every believer remember that it is his duty, if he feels such secret anguish or affliction from a sense of his sins, that he cannot extricate himself without some exterior aid, not to neglect the remedy offered him by the Lord; which is, that in order to alleviate his distress, he should use private confession with his pastor, and, to obtain consolation, should privately implore his assistance, whose office it is, both publicly and privately, to comfort the people of God with the doctrine of the gospel.[6]

Calvin admitted that another person may serve as well as a pastor in hearing the confession, but he preferred the penitent to trust in the minister.

> . . . James, by not expressly appointing any one into whose bosom we should disburden ourselves, leaves us quite at liberty to confess to any member of the church who shall appear most suitable; yet, since the pastors must generally be considered more proper than others, we ought chiefly to make choice of them.[7]

In this confession to a pastor, there was no obligation that all should do it but only individuals who suffered from great anguish and guilt. Ministers were not to lay any yoke upon the conscience in this matter. Neither was anyone bound to enumerate all one's sins. The penitent judged what was to be revealed for the consolation of the soul, and one's liberty in this was to be stoutly defended by the ministers.

So far as frequency was concerned, Calvin wished that Christians would present themselves to their pastor whenever they desired to partake of the Lord's Supper. Here, in freedom, those who were experiencing distress of conscience could be consoled and those requiring it, admonished. But there was no necessity for confession unless it was desired or indicated.

The other kind of private confession was based on Matthew 5:23-24: "So if you are offering your gift at the altar, and there remember that your brother has something against you, leave your gift there before the altar and go; first be reconciled to your brother, and then come and offer your gift." In this case, confession was made directly to the offended person in order that a state of charity might be restored between the two. If the offended "brother" happened to be the whole church, then confession was to be made before it and forgiveness sought, as was the practice in early Christendom.[8]

Calvin does not explicitly deal with the seal of confession in his writings, but his emphasis upon the penitents *privately* imploring the assistance of their pastor and *privately* confessing their sins indicates that he upheld it and recognized it as an inherent part of private confession. He encouraged those with doubts about their forgiveness to disclose this *secretly* to the pastor so that they might be reassured. On the other hand, Calvin's stress upon public confession of public sins (the category under which most crimes would fall) shows what his advice would have been to any lawbreaker who confided in him. Whether or not Calvin would have himself made public the offense if the criminal did not, and what course Calvin would have taken if called to testify about the contents of a confession, remains open to question.

Some hints about his possible actions are contained in his commentary on Matthew 18:15 ("If your brother sins against you, go and tell him his fault, between you and him alone. . . .").

The design of this [instruction] . . . is, to hinder charity from being violated under the pretence of fervent zeal. As the greater part of men are driven by ambition to publish with excessive eagerness the faults of their brethren, Christ seasonably meets this fault by enjoining us to cover the faults of brethren, as far as lies in our power.

This applied only to private offenses, however. He went on to say:

If any man shall *offend* against the whole Church, Paul enjoins that he be publicly reproved, so that even *elders* shall not be spared . . . (I Timothy 5:20). . . . The distinction, therefore, which Christ expressly lays down, ought to be kept in mind, that no man may bring disgrace upon *his brother,* by rashly, and without necessity, divulging secret offences.[9]

It seems fair to conclude that Calvin, unlike Luther, would not have been scrupulous about protecting the confidences of a public offender. However, when a private offender confessed, Calvin probably mentioned the matter to no one else.

Reformed Churches and the Right to Silence. Later references to the seal of confession in the Reformed Churches are few. One stands out. In the Synod of 1612, of the Reformed Church of France, the seal of confession is explicitly recognized. The deliverance states that, except in cases of *lèse majesté,* "ministers are forbidden to disclose to the magistrates crimes declared by those who come to him for counsel and consolation . . . lest sinners be hindered from coming to repentance, and from making a free confession of their faults."[10] The significant point here is that this was an official action of a court of the church, not an unofficial recommendation. Perhaps just as significant is the date of the action. It was taken during those few years when the Huguenots were enjoying a brief respite from their persecutions in France and were, for the time being, a growing, prosperous church. After the Edict of Nantes was revoked in 1685, the Huguenots no longer possessed the luxury of the privilege of silence.

The seal of confession is still recognized occasionally by contemporary descendants of the Reformers of Geneva. John Watson (Ian Maclaren), a Presbyterian, in his Yale Lectures, *The Cure of Souls* (1896), advises that the pastor is to avoid every temptation to mere curiosity and meddlesomeness, and to treat confidences as inviolably sacred.[11] Reformed pastors on the Continent still promise at their consecration to "keep secret those confessions which may be made for the quieting of conscience."[12] Several American church courts such as the Presbytery of Newark (United Presbyterian Church in the U.S.A.) in 1955 and the Synod of Virginia (Presbyterian Church in the United States) in 1961 have reminded the ministers under their jurisdiction of their right to silence.

One such recognition of need is contained in the Report of the Assembly's Committee on the Minister and His Work, adopted by the 1962 General Assembly of the Presbyterian Church in the United States. It reads:

> In 1961 it was called to the attention of this Committee that a minister in one of our Synods testified willingly in an alienation of affection suit. It was discovered during the course of the court proceedings that in that particular state there is no law giving a minister immunity or legal protection when it comes to court matters. When a minister is called upon to testify under these conditions he has but two courses of action: 1. To say: "I don't recall," thus leaving himself [open] to a perjury charge, or 2. To throw himself upon the mercy of the court and say something to the effect that: "I received this information in confidence and cannot share it with you." This answer places the minister in the hands of the presiding judge, who may dismiss him, or take legal action against him.
>
> It is the opinion of the Committee that the above is a matter which should be called to the attention in each case of the

Synod with the suggestion that it be referred to the State Council of Churches, or other similar organization involving other denominations.[13]

The recommendation of the committee is sound. The problem is interdenominational. Where a state does not recognize a pastor's right to silence, action for this recognition can best be taken by the denominations working cooperatively.

Recent General Assembly Actions. In 1981, in response to the Ron Salfen case, both the General Assembly of the United Presbyterian Church in the U.S.A. and the General Assembly of the Presbyterian Church in the U.S. reaffirmed previous stands on privileged communication. The United Presbyterians voted affirmatively on this statement: "That all ministers under the jurisdiction of the United Presbyterian Church in the United States of America are hereby instructed that it is their spiritual and professional duty to hold in confidence all matters revealed to them in their counseling ministry, and that being called to testify in a court of law does not negate this sacred obligation, the law of God being prior to the laws of human courts."[14]

The PCUS General Assembly reaffirmed its 1968 action: "The nature of this office is such that a minister is under obligation not to reveal communications given to him in confidence without the authority of the person revealing the confidence." It stated further, "Being called to testify in a court of law does not negate this sacred obligation, the law of God being prior to the law of human courts."[15]

Chapter VIII / CONFESSION IN THE FREE CHURCH TRADITION

The free churches, represented largely by the Anabaptist movement—Baptists, Mennonites, Moravians, and Brethren, for example—were a significant third force alongside Lutheran and Reformed Churches, in the Reformation. The movement originated in Zurich under the influence of Huldreich Zwingli, though he broke with them in 1525 and became identified with the reformed churches (see chapter 7).

Among the major characteristics of the movement are radical biblicism, believer's baptism by immersion, pacifism, and a view of the church as a disciplined fellowship of believers.

It is this latter teaching that forms the basis for an understanding of confession in the context of the free church experience. It means that there was no auricular confession to clergy, as was found in the Catholic or Anglican traditions. Sin was to be confessed in prayer to God, whose grace could be depended on to free the penitent of all guilt. Those persons wishing to do so were free to talk personally with the "shepherd" or pastor of the community, who would pray with the individual and give advice or counsel. The shepherd, however, had no power or authority over the soul or conscience of any person.

The Anabaptist Confession of Schleitheim (1527) stresses

that the inner life of the congregation is entrusted to the care of "one shepherd, according to the Pauline arrangement, who was to perform all of the spiritual duties."[1] Within this community of faith, members having some grievance against one another were encouraged to confess their faults to one another, on the pattern described in Matthew 18:15-20. Still, among the duties of pastors was "to admonish and teach, to warn, to discipline, to ban in the church . . . and in all things to see to the care of the body of Christ, in order that it may be built up and developed, and the mouth of the slanderer be stopped."[2]

While the Schleitheim Confession exercised greater influence in the spread of the radical Anabaptist movement across Europe, the "Discipline of the Church at Rattenberg" (1527) is more explicit about the exercise of discipline:

> In the third place: when a brother or sister leads a disorderly life it shall be punished: if he does so publicly [he] shall be kindly admonished before all the brethren (Gal. 2, 6; I Cor. 5; II Thess. 3); if it is secret it shall be punished in secret, according to the command of Christ (Matt. 18). . . .
>
> In the ninth place: what is officially done among the brethren and sisters in the brotherhood [or "is judged"] shall not be made public before the world. . . .[3]

The concept of discipline contained in these teachings made the authority of the church dependent on the voluntary loyalty of the members of the local congregation. The congregation was a self-disciplining "brotherhood." Balthasar Hubmaier (1481-1528) published a treatise in 1527 in which he went into some detail on the matter of discipline, writing in the form of a catechetical dialogue between "Leonard" and "John":

Leonard: What is fraternal discipline?

John: When one sees his brother sin, he should go to him in love and admonish him fraternally and privately to leave off such sin. If he does leave off, his soul is won. If he does not, then two or three witnesses should be taken, and he may be admonished before them a second time. If he yields it is well—if not the church should hear of it. He is brought before her and admonished a third time. If he leaves off his sin the church has won his soul.

Leonard: Where does the church get its authority?

John: From Christ's command, given in Matt. xviii.18, John xx.23.

Leonard: By what right may one brother use his authority over another?

John: By the baptismal vow, which subjects everyone to the church and all its members, according to the word of Christ.

Leonard: Suppose the admonished sinner will not correct his course?

John: Then the church has the power and right to exclude and excommunicate him, as a perjurer and apostate.

Leonard: What is excommunication?

John: It is exclusion and separation to such an extent that no fellowship is held with such a person by Christians, whether in speaking, eating, drinking, grinding, baking or in any other way, but he is treated as a heathen and a publican, that is, as an offensive, disorderly and venomous man, who is bound and delivered over to Satan. He is to be avoided and shunned, lest the entire visible church be evil spoken of, disgraced and dishonoured by his company, and corrupted by his example, instead of being startled and made afraid by his punishment, so that they will mortify their sins. For as truly as God lives what the church admits or excludes on earth is admitted or excluded above.

Leonard: What are grounds for exclusion?

John: Unwillingness to be reconciled with one's brother, or to abstain from sin.[4]

It is clear from what has been said that the hearing of penitential confession in the free church tradition is a function of the congregation or "brotherhood," and only occasionally of the pastor. The act of "absolution" (Anabaptists would not use the term) is a function of the congregation or of the person offended by the sinful act. This tradition continues among some free churches, such as the Amish and conservative Mennonite and Brethren groups.

Among Baptists, the most numerous of the present-day free churches, the practice of congregational discipline was never quite as strong as it was among their early forebears. Still, church record books of the seventeenth and eighteenth centuries are replete with accounts of members of Baptist congregations who were subject to discipline. These methods broke down considerably during the nineteenth century and gradually disappeared.[5] Still, among Baptists in the United States and Canada the ideal, if not the practice, of congregational discipline is professed. For example, in 1921 the fundamentalist Baptist Bible Union adopted articles of faith which read in part:

> We believe that a church of Christ is a congregation of baptized believers (a) associated by a covenant of faith and fellowship of the gospel; . . . (d) exercising gifts, rights and privileges invested in them by His word; . . . (g) we hold that the local church has the absolute right of self government, free from the interference of any hierarchy of individuals or organizations; and that the one and only superintendent is Christ, through the Holy Spirit; . . . (i) on all matters of membership, of polity, or government, of discipline, of benevolence, the will of the local church is final.[6]

The Southern Baptist Convention adopted a similar, but far less specific, statement in 1925 under the title "Report of Committee on Baptist Faith and Message," which continues to exercise considerable influence in deliberations of that Convention. It says, in part:

A church of Christ is a congregation of baptized believers associated by covenant in the faith and fellowship of the gospel; observing the ordinances of Christ, governed by his law, and exercising the gifts, rights and privileges invested in them by His word, and seeking to extend the Gospel to the ends of the earth.[7]

The free church tradition of the church as a self-disciplining community, where penitence is a communal event and where absolution is an act of the congregation, raises questions which are especially problematical regarding the extension of the privilege. Are confessions made in a church meeting or trial covered by the privilege? Should they be? Clearly in the Mennonite and early Anabaptist tradition a seal of secrecy was placed on "what is officially done [or 'judged'] among the brethren and sisters in the brotherhood."[8] There is no case law upon which to base a judgment. There is one case in which the judge found that there is no confessional discipline enjoined by a Baptist church, and that therefore the Arkansas privilege statute did not apply to a Baptist pastor called as a witness.[9] In an 1818 Massachusetts case[10] it was held that the defendant's penitential confessions to fellow members of his church were not privileged; therefore the content was evidence to be given the court. The issue here was whether a public confession before a congregation had any claim of privilege. As far as this writer can determine no court has ever held that it does.

The only known recent case to approach the question is Reutkemeier v. Nolte, where communications made to the Session (governing body) of a Presbyterian congregation were found to be privileged by the Iowa Supreme Court (see chapter 7). Thus, it would appear that whether or not a church trial is privileged would hinge on the discipline of the church regarding trials, especially in those states where the "discipline enjoined" test is a part of the statute.

In Reutkemeier v. Nolte the court did not distinguish between a "confession" and a "trial," though there are some obvious differences—even when the trial involves a confession. A confessional act is basically voluntary, even if enjoined by the discipline of the church; a trial occurs upon the initiative of the judicatory at a set time and place. In a confession there is a clear penitential intent; at a trial, such an intent may be entirely absent. No written record is kept of what transpires in a confessional act; a trial often leaves a written record which may form the basis for an appeal to higher judicatories. (Early Baptist practice included a right of appeal from the local church to the area association and from there to a general convention of Baptist churches.[11])

This problem would never have arisen for early Anabaptist churches because, as a highly persecuted and unpopular religious minority, they had almost no rights before the law. Further, as a matter of doctrine they rejected the authority of the state to do anything for or against them other than to provide a basic protection for the free exercise of religion. They would not resort to civil magistrates for any cause.

For modern-day free churches the situation is quite different and the legal protections afforded churches which are self-disciplining communities are very limited indeed, insofar as the statutes covering the subject at hand are concerned. There is no basis in law, as it now stands, for making any claim for confidentiality in the matter of a conversation heard by a group. In fact, the very act of making the information known to a group is prima facie evidence that the matter is not confidential. No matter what the discipline of the church says about making confession in the presence of the congregation—even if the congregation is bound by a seal of secrecy after the manner of the Anabaptists at Rattenberg—North American jurisprudence is not likely to exclude the content of such a confession from testimony should such a case arise. At least, any court that did so would act without precedent.

Some rather serious constitutional questions arise in this regard. If the protection of the privilege is denied to churches having no tradition of private auricular confession, but allowed to those which do, does this amount to an "establishment of religion" or to an abridgment of "the free exercise thereof" within the meaning of the First Amendment? Or does such a differentiation based on a particular doctrine of confession or a particular kind of church governance violate the rights of the unprotected to "equal protection under the law" guaranteed by the Fourteenth Amendment? These are untried questions.

The disciplinary act of churches may also become the subject of litigation. In one case, a Mennonite who was excommunicated and "shunned" sued the church. The Supreme Court of Pennsylvania ruled that, the First Amendment "free exercise of religion" guarantee not withstanding, the church was subject to legal action.[12] In that case, the plaintiff, Robert L. Bear, complained that, as a part of being "shunned" by church members under the order of their bishops, his business was in danger of collapse since he was not able to hire workers, obtain loans, or sell his products in his predominantly Mennonite community. In addition, he said his family was coming apart because his wife and children were not allowed to speak to him or have physical contact with him, under fear of being excommunicated themselves. While not ruling on the substance of the case, the Pennsylvania Supreme Court overturned a lower court action which dismissed Bear's suit. The higher court said Bear is entitled to sue for relief.

Several free churches have adopted strong policy statements on privileged communications. One of these is

the American Baptist Convention, whose executive committee of the General Board affirmed such a statement in
1978. It says, in part:

> The effective pastoral counseling of the ministry depends
> upon the assurance of those who seek it that the information
> they reveal in confidence to their pastoral counselor may be
> given with full freedom. The American Baptist Church in the
> U.S.A. expresses its conviction that such confidential, spiritual
> communications to its ministers should have the status of
> privileged communications. . . .
>
> The American Baptist Church in the U.S.A. further
> declares that, whether or not appropriate statutes are enacted,
> it is a principle with us that any of our number who receive
> confidential information in the course of responding to a
> request for spiritual counseling is not morally obligated to
> disclose it without consent of the other party.[13]

Chapter IX / THE
JEWISH EXPERIENCE

There has been no distinct confessional tradition within historic Judaism, at least since the demise of the temple priesthood. The present role of the rabbi as spiritual advisor and counselor has emerged as a fairly recent North American development and this role is still evolving under the dual influences of *demands from members of congregations* and the *Protestant pastoral role.*

The idea of confession and forgiveness of God grew within the religious thought of Judaism over several centuries. In the most primitive period God was understood as an offended diety needing to be appeased, and the cultus provided the means for doing this. As the idea of "chosenness" grew and Israel learned the meaning of her covenant relationship with God, the primitive belief matured into an understanding of loving-kindness. God was unwilling to hold the trespasses of his people against them if they made their confession and returned to what was right and good. In its mature form Judaism was transformed by an understanding of the transcendence and sovereignty of God and by the knowledge that he forgives not only because of his tenderheartedness but because of his power and authority—an authority that he chooses to use to deliver his people as far from their trespasses as the east is from the west.

This growth in understanding is seen in the expanding insights of the prophets. For Hosea, sin was a violation of the law of God. For Jeremiah it was a breach of God's covenant, calling for a confession and a return to the ways of righteousness. For Isaiah, sin was a violation of the holiness of God, an affront to his majesty, requiring submission to his judgment in repentance. A synthesization of these themes emerges over time into a distinctly Jewish confessional viewpoint.

In the Hebrew scriptures, sinners seek God's mercy and receive the remission of sin by following the mourning customs: fasting and weeping, rending the garments, shaving the head, adorning themselves with sackcloth and ashes, all signs of confession and repentance.

In the period following the Exile great emphasis was placed on the observance of the Day of Atonement and offerings were made at the temple for the forgiveness of sins. From this act of general confession we gain the first signs of the idea of confession to the priest from which the practice of individual offerings requiring individual confessions emerges (Lev. 5:1-5; 16:21).

Penitential acts were carried out by the temple priesthood in ancient times, but this practice was lost with the demise of the priesthood. As the influence of the rabbis increased some of the ancient roles of the priesthood fell upon the rabbi, and it became common for people to go to the rabbi for instruction as to what penitence might be appropriate for their sins. As teachers of the tradition, the rabbi would then give advice or instruction. Coincidentally, however, the act of consulting about what was required involved a hearing of confession, though the hearing is clearly not penitential in nature and is not discussed in specific terms in rabbinic literature. One commentator entertains the question,

How is to be understood what the Talmudists say, that he is wanton who proclaims his sins particularly? This is to be understood of him who tells everyone how he has sinned. But it is allowable to tell a just and modest man anything about his sins, in order that he may teach him how to make his repentance.[1]

Regardless of what tradition does or does not exist concerning the role of the rabbi as spiritual advisor or counselor, the modern rabbi in the United States is increasingly considered a source of personal and spiritual help. In addition to his roles as scholar and instructor in the traditions of the faith, today's rabbi is sought out by those needing advice and assistance. Rabbi Mordecai Waxman makes this quite clear:

In communities where clearly there has been an increase in family tensions and where the family structure has been much affected and where, in addition, the parental figures or grandparental figures have been removed from the community so that levels of authority on a vertical level have declined, the rabbi is likely, more and more, to be called upon for counseling functions. It is already clear that counselling is a major aspect of the rabbinic role and that a great many rabbis feel that they need far more training in this area. . . . The seminaries ultimately will have to recognize that with the family structure as it is and the number of disturbed children who result, there is a very serious need for better training of the rabbis in the performance of their functions and that the amount of time that is given to this training is today inadequate.[2]

In a similar vein, Rabbi Harold Saperstein sees the role of the rabbi as counselor and pastor in this way:

[The] fact is that many people will turn to a rabbi specifically because he represents a structure of values. Similarly, in his ministry to people in relation to marriage, grief, illness, life-cycle ceremonies, the rabbi can have a profound influence and render a valuable service. He must, of course, have a basic understanding of modern counselling techniques; but he must also bring the wisdom of Jewish insight and experience. That is a special function which no one else can do as well.[5]

What Waxman and Saperstein observe is born out by recent case law, which indicates that rabbis are finding themselves increasingly drawn into the role of counselor and spiritual advisor and ending up being asked to recount the contents of their conversations in court. The question of the privilege in relation to conversations between a rabbi and those whom he or she is called on to counsel has been a factor in several civil cases.

In a case heard prior to the liberalization of the New York statute, a husband and wife received a message from a rabbi whom they had never met, asking them to come to see him. This rabbi made the request because another rabbi, who had known the couple elsewhere and who knew the couple was having marital trouble, asked the New York rabbi to try to accomplish a reconciliation. The couple met the rabbi in his study at Forest Hills Jewish Center where the rabbi was "spiritual advisor." The attempts at reconciliation were not successful. In the litigation that ensued the rabbi was called as a witness.[4] After being sworn, the rabbi exerted the claim of privilege for his communications with the couple. Circuit Judge Harold J. Crawford held that the conversations the rabbi had with the couple were privileged and that the rabbi should not be allowed to testify concerning them.

In large part Judge Crawford's decision was based on a letter from the New York Board of Rabbis, dated May 17, 1961, and quoted in the opinion:

> The New York Board of Rabbis deem it essential for the proper work of the Rabbi in the community that any confidence reposed in him by a husband and wife, individually or jointly, or anyone else who has come to him for counseling,

not be divulged, and we hope that the Court will sustain this action. Otherwise the confidential role of the Rabbi in counselling would be completely violated, to the detriment of those who seek his guidance.

This case is important on several scores. First, it extends the privilege to a rabbi in a state where the statute at the time was quite restrictive, containing language relating to priest-penitent privileges, "confession" and "discipline enjoined by the church." Second, the judge specifically noted that the initiative for the consultation came from the rabbi and not from the couple, holding that "it matters not who initiates the meeting." Third, the content of the communication, while not inquired into by the court, apparently did not involve conduct which was culpable, and possibly not sinful—thus requiring no "confession" even if the religious discipline of the parties in the case had required it.

The second case did not end on so positive a note insofar as the privilege is concerned. It arose in California in 1965 and also involved a rabbi engaged in attempting to reconcile differences in a marriage. It was also heard under a traditional statute, just a year before the California law was expanded in scope. In this case the judge held that the statute's language regarding "confession in the course of discipline enjoined by the church" does not apply to a religious or spiritual advisor acting as a marriage counselor. It is not clear from the opinion whether this finding was related to the fact that the clergyman was a *rabbi*, though the point seems to be that the function was that of *marriage counselor*. In his ruling, the judge noted: "We think this result is regrettable for reasons of public policy . . . but the wording of the statute leaves us no choice."[5]

A survey of current statutes indicates that in twenty-seven states "rabbi" is named specifically as a category of clergy expressly covered by the law. In twenty-three states, the generic term "clergyman" is used and may be presumed to include rabbis. Only Iowa has a statute whose language is less inclusive, referring only to a "minister of the gospel or priest of any denomination."

There are some continuing questions that require the vigilance of rabbis—indeed, of all clergy—as cases arise in which they are called to testify. Some courts have interpreted state laws quite narrowly, especially on the issue of the "discipline enjoined" language present in a number of the statutes. In some cases, the privilege is recognized when the specific religious tradition (a) *requires* that the clergy absolutely preserve the "seal of the confessional" and (b) *requires* that confession be made to clergy. In a few cases the privilege has been denied to those whose religious tradition does not meet these two "discipline enjoined" tests. In a strict construction of the language of traditional statutes, is there a denial of equal protection guaranteed under the Fourteenth Amendment to the Constitution of the United States? Or is there an abridgment of the "free exercise of religion" clause of the First Amendment? In a state where legal precedent has recognized the claim of clergy where there is a "discipline enjoined by the church" but denied the claim to those religious communities not having such a requirement, is there a violation of the "establishment of religion" prohibition of the First Amendment? These questions have never been litigated. One could only surmise what the result of such tests might be.

Chapter X/THE
CHURCHES REEXAMINE
CONFESSION

One of the signs of our times within Protestantism is a renewed interest in confession. For many years it has lain dormant in the churches of the Reformation. Now, they are reexamining its biblical warrant and its helpfulness in the ministry of the church to society. A typical report is one carried by Religious News Service, originating in Toronto, Ontario:

> Confession is as beneficial to Protestants as to Roman Catholics and should be made to a minister or trusted Christian friend, a United Church of Canada committee suggested here in a report entitled "Church Membership, Doctrine and Practice in the United Church of Canada."
>
> Calvin, the report said, supported voluntary, private confession and, while advocating that a man is free to confess to any suitable member of the church, said that "since pastors must be considered more proper for this than others, we ought chiefly to make choice of them."
>
> Luther, it added, also taught confession must be voluntary and private, saying that "if you are too proud to confess your sins, we conclude that you are no Christian."[1]

Most of the interest seems to have begun during and since World War II. It broke out most prominently in 1956 at the evangelical church assembly held in Frankfurt, Germany, where the theme was treated by a special study group and where approximately thirty places were set up throughout the city where private confessions could be heard. At one site seventy people came for confession in one night and two more places had to be hastily improvised. So many people came to another location that the confessor had to remain at his post until midnight to accommodate them all.[2]

Three Reasons Why. Why this renewed interest in an institution that most Protestants had previously associated with Rome? Three reasons can be given rather quickly. In the first place, the resurgent interest in confession can be correlated to some extent with the growth of the liturgical movement within Protestantism. Within the Anglican, Lutheran, and Reformed Churches, there has been a growing interest in recovering the worship heritage of the church. When this restudy turned to the sacraments, the place of confession was reevaluated. The sacrament of penance was one of the seven sacraments of the church prior to the Reformation. Should it not be given sacramental status again? Some Anglo-Catholics would like to restore it to the list along with the other lost four. But even if it is not of sacramental value, does not private confession have a legitimate place in the total worship life of the church? Many maintain that it does. Furthermore, in the restudy of the sacrament of the Lord's Supper, the practice of private confession is being considered as a recommended act before partaking of Holy Communion. The renewed interest in worship and church life, then, has led at least one segment of Protestantism to take a fresh look at private confession.

In the second place, this new interest in confession can be partially attributed to the increasing secularism of life in today's world. There is much guilt today in the lives of people within and without the church, and probably more guilt for those who hold moral values which society takes less and less seriously. A full life in the world, even for the conscientious Christian, means more compromises, more questionable actions, more sense of individual and corporate sin. This guilt must be removed and the person restored to wholeness. Some people search for restoration through psychotherapy, but many others, with a more profound understanding of the reason for their estrangement, come for confession. And this confession must be to a person; the general confession and assurance of pardon of corporate worship seem too vague and abstract. There are specific sins to be confessed and they must be confessed to a specific person.

The third reason follows from the second. Increasingly, the Protestant minister is called on today to act in the role of a confessor, whether he desires that role or not. And this new role has caused him and the church to consider the matter in a new light. On the one hand he feels threatened by the psychotherapist, who is much better trained to root out hidden causes of guilt, hostility, and anxiety. On the other hand, he knows that the ultimate answer to human estrangement is not to be found in psychotherapy but in Christian forgiveness. Out of this tension have come books, seminary courses and departments, and special schools, all designed to train the pastor to handle more adequately those problems brought by parishioners and others—problems which often lead formally or informally to confession. In other words, the world has forced the church to take a new look at confession because the world has come to the church's door, searching for forgiveness.

Bonhoeffer's Reexamination. Several theologians in particular represent the current reexamination of confession. One is Dietrich Bonhoeffer, a Lutheran martyr of the Hitler regime. As a pastor and teacher in the confessing church, he considered the place of confession in the Christian community.[3] Bonhoeffer believed that it was only the pious fellowship that permitted no one to be a sinner. The true Christian community would recognize a man for what he was. Christ, he said, gave to his followers the authority to hear the confession of sin and to forgive sin in his name (John 20:23). Confession need not be in the presence of the whole congregation; it may be made to any Christian brother, for the sinner meets the whole congregation in the brother to whom confession is made and from whom forgiveness is received.

Although Bonhoeffer says that confession as an act is complete in itself, it serves the Christian community especially as a preparation for the common reception of Holy Communion. Not only should there be an asking of mutual forgiveness by those within the community before they take the Lord's Supper together, but where there is deep anxiety and trouble over one's own sins, where the certainty of forgiveness is sought, there should be the invitation in the name of Jesus to come to confession. In this way, the joy of the day of Communion can be most fully experienced.

In only one place does Bonhoeffer mention the seal of confession. In speaking of a person hearing our confession, he says: "He hears the confession of our sins in Christ's stead and he forgives our sins in Christ's name. He keeps the secret of our confession as God keeps it. When I go to my brother to confess, I am going to God."[4] For Bonhoeffer, as for his spiritual teacher, Luther, the confession was inviolable.

He also follows Luther on a closely related subject: what it means to tell the truth. Bonhoeffer says that truthfulness does not mean the disclosure of everything that exists.

God Himself made clothes for man (Gen. 3.21); and this means that *in statu corruptionis* many things in man are to remain concealed, and that if it is too late to eradicate evil, it is at least to be kept hidden. Exposure is cynical; and even if the cynic appears to himself to be specially honest, or if he sets himself up to be a fanatical devotee of truth, he nevertheless fails to achieve the truth which is of decisive importance, namely, the truth that since the Fall there has been a need also for concealment and secrecy. . . . In my view "telling the truth" means saying how something is in reality, *i.e.*, respect for secrecy, confidence and concealment. "Betrayal," for example, is not truth; nor are frivolity, cynicism, etc. What is concealed must be disclosed only at confession, *i.e.*, before God.[5]

This very revealing statement seems to indicate that Bonhoeffer would have refused to testify concerning the contents of a confession if asked to do so by the authorities of the state. He might even have gone as far as Luther in denying that he knew anything about the matter at all.

Thurneysen's Corrective. Another representative of this reexamination of confession is Eduard Thurneysen, pastor and professor at Basel. Standing within the Reformed tradition, he views with some skepticism the suggestions of those who would go to extremes in reinstituting private confession in Protestantism. Confession, he says, is simply the acknowledgment of sin—owning up to something definite that we have done and for which we are responsible. Its purpose is to seek forgiveness. But only God can forgive. This is the message of Jesus Christ. God, who is merciful beyond all comprehension, offers forgiveness as a free gift. And God does this without any preliminary acknowledgment of sins on our part. Evangelical confession differs from Catholic confession in that it takes place only as an action subsequent to what Christ has already done for us and subsequent to what makes our confession possible in the first place.[6]

But this forgiveness must be imparted. So Christ has

deposited his word of forgiveness in the church. On the authority of Christ it pronounces that word of forgiveness. This he ordered his disciples to do when he said: "Receive the Holy Spirit. If you forgive the sins of any, they are forgiven; if you retain the sins of any, they are retained" (John 20:22-23). Within the church, Christ has established three places where his word of forgiveness is issued and its power proven: baptism, preaching, and the Communion table. The confessional is not included. Members of the evangelical church have no commission to establish it anew in any form. Rather, the worship service of the church becomes the site of true, evangelical confession.

However, when the right hour comes, there may also be private confession before a Christian neighbor, or brother or sister in the church. This cannot be required or organized. It is a ministry which is not only practiced by the pastor but also and primarily is reciprocated among church members. In essence, this evangelical private confession is no different from the general confession of the congregation —both are concerned with the forgiveness of sins. In both private and public confession Christ uncovers and forgives the sin and thereby builds his church. But in private confession, the call to forgiveness is now directed to one single person, whereas it had been directed to everyone in the preaching, Holy Communion, and prayer of the congregation.

In summary, Thurneysen says that private confession is genuine when it comes entirely from the grace of Christ and is illuminated by that grace. It takes place within the church, for here we receive Christ's word of forgiveness. It cannot be organized nor is it necessary to confess to a pastor, although he may frequently be the person sought out. There can be no set hours nor any prescribed place nor any standard set of furnishings for the room. It is all a matter of grace, and grace is free—not tied to location or practice or liturgy. Grace, like miracles, cannot be brought about by human measures.

Tournier and Mowrer. Two Protestant laymen—one a psychiatrist, the other a psychologist—have also reminded the churches of the value of confession. Paul Tournier, the Swiss psychiatrist, gives a personal testimony to its effect in his life.

> I myself had for a long time a religious life which was rather intellectual and theoretical; I was a militant Church member; I truly believed not only in God and in Jesus Christ, but also in the Holy Spirit, the communion of saints, the forgiveness of sins, and the holy Catholic Church. But that, for me, was a belief rather than a living experience until the day when I met men who simply and honestly confessed their sins.
> Those men showed me the way, not by exhortation but by their example in my presence. I threw myself wholeheartedly into the regular practice of confession, moved by an inner impetus and not in order to fulfill a legalistic condition. The whole climate of my life changed. I was at last experiencing what I had known for a long time. "Now I understand," I said, "what the action of the Holy Spirit, the conviction of sin and the experience of grace really are."[7]

Tournier goes on to tell of the spiritual ministry that then opened before him. People in large numbers came and as the result of an absolutely concrete confession found true freedom. Its effect was not limited to the religious experience of freedom from guilt, but there came as well the cure of a physical or psychological illness. And the cures came rapidly. Sometimes in less than an hour he would notice the same release from psychological tension which ordinarily would have been expected only after months of therapy.

O. Hobart Mowrer, then research professor of psychology at the University of Illinois, also reminded the churches and their pastors of the connection between guilt and mental illness, and between confession (plus expiation) and mental health. From long study and research he concluded that much of mental illness is the result of real guilt, rather than imagined wrongdoings. And the proper way to handle real guilt is not by psychotherapy but by confession and expiation.

Mowrer felt that Protestantism had embraced a theology which put the problem of personal guilt beyond the scope of religion. In effect, it fostered the development of secular psychotherapy in general and Freudian psychoanalysis in particular. But analytic treatment and theory did not lessen our woes; rather, they became worse. Today many psychologists are looking to religion with renewed hope and urgency. The problem has been that in the past personality disorder was looked upon as basically an *illness—mental illness.* Now, psychologists are persuaded that the problem is fundamentally moral, that the guilt which is so obviously central in psychopathology is real rather than false. Only a moral attack can be successful with this kind of problem. Mowrer says:

> We had hoped that an easy solution might be found for personal evil; and we have tried both the doctrine of "cheap grace" (in religion) and the strategy of denying the reality of sin and guilt altogether (in psychoanalysis), but neither has worked. And so today there is a growing readiness to accept the verdict that "therapy," or "salvation," is possible only at great cost: the cost of self-revelation, deep contrition, and a radically changed way of life.[8]

If the viewpoint which Mowrer projected gains wide acceptance, it could radically change the job description of the average Protestant minister. Much more time than is now given would be spent on the cure of souls. Logically, we could also expect the minister's right to silence to be called into question more often than in the past.

The Experience at Taizé. Taizé is a religious community of ordained and lay brothers—a little village near Cluny in Burgundy. Its members are drawn from the various reformed churches of both the Calvinist and the Lutheran traditions in Europe; its purpose is to bring together "men dedicated to a common service of Jesus Christ in the Church and the world."

Confession is practiced as a part of the discipline of the community. Max Thurian, a pastor in residence, has written of his experience and that of the community as this act has been observed during the years.[9] While he takes care in pointing out its blessings, he also does not neglect its dangers and hindrances. Let us concern ourselves with them for a moment.

There is a danger to the person who comes to confession that he will depend on it too much. Some people are unwilling to grow up in their Christian life. They live like parasites on the ministry of the cure of souls. Their pastor is consulted on even trivial matters. Such a dependence on confession must be discouraged.

The corresponding danger to the pastors is that their time is monopolized by folks who seek their counsel too often. They owe a duty to all members of the church. Sometimes, they may need to refuse counsel to those who desire it too frequently and who have grown dependent on it. Like wise parents, they must try to set them free by leading them to their spiritual coming-of-age.

One important obstacle to confession is the fear that its secrecy may be betrayed. The confessors must keep secret those confessions made to them for the quieting of conscience. Not only must they keep the words secret, but they must also be careful that by their attitude or gestures they do not betray the confession. Thurian suggests that it would be well for Protestants to study the elaborate precautions taken by the Roman Catholic Church to preserve the seal of confession.

Neither may the pastors share with their spouses any of the contents of a confession or even the fact that it has been made. To encourage the practice of confession among their flock, they must not meet the parishioner at the study in his or her home but rather provide for a place in the church or some independent office where the person will find it easier to unburden his or her heart.

An additional hindrance is that the person who comes to confession may fear that the confessor will always remember the sin confessed and that ordinary everyday relationships with him or her will become a source of embarrassment. While the difficulty is real it can be avoided in several ways, if the confession is made in an atmosphere of simple sincerity. For one thing, pastors should be careful to maintain such control over themselves that they will never, even by the most secret look or gesture, remind the penitent that they are aware of what has been confessed. They should pray that these things be blotted out from their memory. Furthermore, the confessors should pray that the absolution addressed to the penitent may be equally effective in their own mind. The pastors do not take the burden of the sins upon themselves but simply help the penitent bring them to Christ. When they realize their own humble part in this act, they will more easily be able, by God's grace, to blot them out from their memory. The experience of many confessors is that they do, in fact, think of the sins of the penitent only at the moment of confession, in intercession, and when reflecting on the proper spiritual advice to give. Outside of these times, they are able to remain simple and natural.

The Outlook Ahead. As we look to the future two observations seem obvious. One is that private confession will increase within the evangelical churches because of the reasons mentioned earlier. It may very well take the form of informal confession suggested by Thurneysen and practiced in the name of pastoral counseling or family guidance. Or it may, especially in the liturgical churches, take on more of the aspects of the traditional confessional of the Roman Catholic Church. In any event, the church is reexamining the place of confession in twentieth-century culture because its people are seeking a place to find forgiveness. Psychotherapy has been, and still is, providing a way to confess for some who can afford it. But it cannot offer forgiveness. Only the church can offer that, in the name of Christ. The church must not ignore its responsibility to those who come, for they have nowhere else to go.

The second observation is that the seal of confession will become more and more a point of discussion within Protestantism. At least two factors will cause this. One is the increased number of people who are coming to confession, formally or informally. The seal of confession will consequently be called into question more often than in the past, if only on the basis of simple arithmetic. The second factor is more basic. In the past the seal of confession has been recognized by the law as applying only to priests or pastors. (The single exception has been the Presbyterian ruling elder, considered in another chapter.) If the evangelical churches take seriously the Reformation heritage of Luther and Calvin, given contemporary expression by Bonhoeffer and Thurneysen, who assert that confession can be to any brother or sister in the church, how will the seal of confession apply to these lay confessors? Are their lips to remain sealed before the law as those of ordained clergy? Will the courts be willing to recognize as privileged a confession of guilt made to an unordained Christian? If they do not, what is the lay confessor's responsibility for retaining confidences entrusted to him or her? This matter seems very much unsettled in church circles even though the law is quite clear that communications made to lay Christians are not privileged. Perhaps the church will be forced to develop a twentieth-century doctrine of the seal of confession that applies alike to ministers and laity, just as it seems to be developing a contemporary doctrine of the confession itself. Until then, no clear answers can be given to the questions just raised.

Part II/THE LAW AND CONFIDENTIALITY

Chapter XI/SOME
NECESSARY DEFINITIONS

In this section we begin consideration of the legal side—the history, scope, and status of the pastor's right to silence. This means that we must become acquainted with legal terminology. Such language is precise and often cannot be paraphrased without losing some of the essential meaning. So, if these next few pages are full of long quotations, it is only because there seems no good way to get around them.

First, while we have used the term previously, let us see what precisely is meant by the "common law." *Black's Law Dictionary* can help us.

> The common law is that body of law and juristic theory which was originated, developed, and formulated and is administered in England, and has obtained among most of the states and peoples of Anglo-Saxon stock.
>
> As distinguished from law created by the enactment of legislatures, the common law comprises the body of those principles and rules of action, relating to the government and security of persons and property, which derive their authority solely from usages and customs of immemorial antiquity, or from the judgments and decrees of the courts recognizing, affirming, and enforcing such usages and customs; and, in this sense, particularly the ancient unwritten law of England. . . .
>
> As concerns its force and authority in the United States, the

phrase designates that portion of the common law of England
. . . which had been adopted and was in force here at the time
of the Revolution. This, so far as it has not since been expressly
abrogated, is recognized as an organic part of the jurisprudence of most of the United States.[1]

Next, contrast the "common law" with "statute law." The
same source says a statute is

an act of the legislature declaring, commanding, or prohib-
iting something; a particular law enacted and established by
the will of the legislative department of government; the
written will of the legislature, solemnly expressed according to
the forms necessary to constitute it the law of the state. . . .
*This word is used to designate the written law in contradistinction to
the unwritten law.*[2]

A court will render a decision on the basis of the common
law unless the legislature has passed a statute to the
contrary. Even then, the weight of the statute is usually
limited to the express provisions it contains; it is, in legal
terms, strictly construed.

There are several other terms that will come up again and
again in our study of this whole field. Now is the time to
define them. The first is "privilege."

The word "privilege" has a variety of meanings, according to
the connection or context in which it is used; but inherent in
the term is the idea of something apart and distinct from a
common right which pertains to all citizens or exists in all
subjects. . . . "Privilege" has been defined as meaning a right
not enjoyed by all; a right peculiar to an individual or body; a
right peculiar to the person or class of persons on whom it is
conferred, and not possessed by others; a special right or
power conferred or possessed by one or more individuals in
derogation of the general right; an immunity granted by
authority; a peculiar immunity; an immunity held beyond the
course of the law; a right or immunity not enjoyed by others or
by all.[3]

Another term is that much-used word "communication." Legally, it is defined as

the act of communicating. The term also means intelligence, news, that which is communicated or imparted, a written or verbal message; something said by one person to another. It is not restricted, however, to mere words, but includes acts as well, embracing every variety of affairs which can form the subject of negotiation, interviews, or actions between two persons, and every method by which one person can derive impressions or information from the conduct, condition, or language of another.[4]

If this is what is understood as communication, what, then, is meant by a "confidential communication"? The following definition is given:

Confidential communications. Certain classes of communications, passing between persons who stand in a confidential or fiduciary relation to each other (or who, on account of their relative situation, are under a special duty of secrecy or fidelity), which the law will not permit to be divulged, or allow them to be inquired into in a court of justice, for the sake of public policy and the good order of society. The phrase describes only secret communications, the secrecy being enjoined either actually or by implication, and so does not include communications made for the purpose, or with the expectation, of being disclosed, or those made in the presence of others.[5]

Finally, a communication, because of its confidential nature, may be considered legally privileged. This is understood as follows:

Privileged communication. A communication communicated in confidence, privately indorsed, secret, in reliance on secrecy.[6]
The term is employed in the law with two significations. In one sense it signifies oral or printed utterances which are not actionable although defamatory, and in this sense the term is

treated in Libel and Slander §§87-120 [see Appendix at end of book]. In another sense the term "privileged communication" has reference to communications made during the existence of certain confidential relationships recognized by law and not competent to be produced in court during the trial of a case.[7]

There are usually two kinds of privileged communication recognized by law. A communication called absolutely privileged means that no legal action can be taken against the originator even though it is false and made with malicious intent. Such an absolutely privileged statement can be made only by a judge sitting on his bench or by a legislative body. The other type of privileged communication is called qualifiedly privileged. Under this category come those statements made to or by a person in connection with his professional responsibilities in relationships usually recognized as confidential.[8] The main concern of this chapter will be with those confidential relationships ordinarily established in the pastoral work of a minister.

Privilege in General. The law is clear that when persons occupy toward one another certain confidential relations, such as a husband and a wife, they will not be compelled or even allowed to violate the confidence reposed in them by the other party. Public policy (the consideration of the total common good of all) demands that they not testify, without the consent of the other party, to the communications made to them. Even a statute making both parties competent and compellable to testify still cannot open the door to a full inquiry into such privileged communications.

The courts have held that privilege is a matter of statute. The general rule followed is that there is no privilege in the absence of a statute, unless this privilege was granted by the common law. However, authorities disagree about how strictly a statute on privilege should be construed. Some would say that for statements to be privileged, and hence inadmissible as evidence, they must come within the express terms of the statute. But other authorities accord the statutes a broad and liberal construction, so that they may help carry out a long-standing public policy of encouraging uninhibited communication between persons standing in a relation of confidence and trust.[9]

When Communications Are Not Privileged. The mere fact that a communication is regarded as confidential does not render it privileged in a legal sense. The law cannot take into account purely sentimental considerations which might hinder public interests. This means that when the parties stand in no relation which the law considers confidential, a witness cannot be excused or prevented from testifying about matters which were communicated to him. He is not immune even though at the time that the communication was made, both parties understood it to be a purely private conversation spoken in confidence and in reliance on a promise of secrecy.

What this means, for one thing, is that the law does not recognize the legality of lay confession. Protestants place great stress on the doctrine of the priesthood of all believers, which implies that every layperson can serve as confessor to another. But if one lay Christian confesses a sin for which that one could be punished by law to another lay Christian, that confession is not privileged in the courts. The confessor, if called as a witness, would have to testify about its contents. Only if the confessor is a minister, and then only if there is a statute protecting the priest-penitent relationship, is the confession immune from disclosure.

Facts that are plain to the observation of anyone cannot be considered privileged communications. Nor does the privilege extend to a person who by accident or design overhears a privileged communication. Such a third party can be called to testify as to the communication which he saw, heard, or read.[10] We will discuss this point again later as it applies particularly to church secretaries, associate or assistant pastors, and directors of Christian education. Roman Catholic ecclesiastical law states that the seal of confession affects anyone who might accidentally overhear or otherwise have knowledge of communications that passed in the confessional. Civil law has not always recognized this canon as binding.

What Relations, Then, Are Privileged? Under the common law, only two relations were recognized as privileged—those between attorney and client and those between husband and wife. Those which have been added to this list in the meantime, such as the privileged relation between physician and patient, have been granted by statute because they seemed by many states to be in the public interest. In addition, statutes have been enacted in more states strengthening the privileged relationships recognized under the common law. Here are some of the rules governing the recognized privileged relationships before the law, including that of the clergy and the penitent.

ATTORNEY AND CLIENT. The rule about privileged communication between attorney and client was applied at an early period by the English courts and has been upheld for at least the last three centuries. It is a common law privilege that exists independently of statute, but in some states it has been expressed by statute.

While an attorney as such is not considered incompetent as a witness and even may be called to witness for or against a client, the scope of the testimony permitted is limited by the rule of nondisclosure of communications of a professional nature between the attorney and client. This rule, long established by the common law, states that attorneys, counselors, or solicitors are not permitted, and cannot be compelled, to testify as to communications made to them in their professional character by their client, unless the client consents. The rule is based on the grounds of public policy, and the courts must enforce it unless such enforcement is waived by the client. Since these communications are privileged on the basis of public policy, the courts cannot allow the attorneys to disclose them even if they should desire to do so.

The same rule applies to the client as to the attorney. The clients cannot disclose confidential communications made to them by their attorney without the attorney's consent. Where a third person is present and hears the communication, that person is usually judged a competent witness unless he or she happens to be an interpreter or the client's or the attorney's agent. An attorney's clerk has been held to be privileged.[11]

HUSBAND AND WIFE. An established rule of common law, adopted for the protection of the institution of marriage, is that neither party in a marriage may be a witness in favor of or against the other. The purpose of this is to encourage mutual confidences between husband and wife to preserve the marital status. The law considers that a man must be able to impart to his wife, and a woman to her husband, the most critical conditions of his or her affairs with the full assurance that no process of law can compel a violation of the confidence.

Many states have embodied the common law privileges in statutes which, in general, have the same substance as the common law rule, although their wording may vary. When a third person is present and hears the communication, the law does not regard it as privileged and either party may testify to this communication, even though the third party may now be dead. The only significant exception to this rule is the presence of young children who pay no attention to what is being discussed. The communication is then considered privileged. But it is not so considered if the children are older.[12]

PHYSICIAN AND PATIENT. Under the common law a physician called as a witness has no right to decline or refuse to disclose any information on the ground that it was communicated to him or her confidentially by the patient. Nor could the patient, by objection, stop the physician from testifying. This is still the rule unless there is a statute to the contrary.

This condition is deplored by leading jurists and in the profession generally, and, as a result, statutes have been enacted in most states making communications between a physician and patient privileged from compulsory disclosure in courts of justice.

As with other types of privileged communication, the privilege does not apply if the communication is made in the presence of a third person. The exception occurs when a third person is present in order to assist in the healing of the patient, or in the communications between the physician and the patient. For instance, the spouse of a patient can testify as to treatments given; so, too, may an ambulance driver. But the partner of a physician is incompetent to testify and, by implication, so is a personal nurse if the statute so states. Otherwise, the nurse is deemed a competent witness. The statutes apply only to physicians or surgeons duly authorized to practice their profession under the laws of the state. They do not apply to chiropractors, dentists, druggists and drug clerks, and veterinary surgeons. As is the case with other privileged relationships, the patient may waive the privilege by voluntarily testifying to the privileged matters but cannot be compelled to do so, even though the statute does not expressly grant immunity to the patient but only to the physician.[13]

OTHER PRIVILEGED RELATIONSHIPS. Other relationships which may be considered privileged, usually depending on whether there is an express statute to that effect, are as follows: Communications of state secrets to public officers and employees are held privileged. So, too, are communications by informers to public officials, including the prosecuting attorney. Many states and the federal government have statutes that make statements and returns of tax papers privileged against disclosure by forbidding divulgence of tax information, records, and reports of an individual. In most jurisdictions, jurors are privileged and shall not be questioned concerning any verdict they have delivered. Grand jurors always have the right to keep silent. Communications between associate counsel are ordinarily privileged as well.[14]

Normally, the courts are very reluctant to grant privileges, and the tendency is to limit them as much as possible within the expressed working of the statutes. There is also little tendency in the courts at the present time to extend the privileged relationship to new professional groups, such as marriage counselors and clinical psychologists. Privileges, except in the instances already specified, are generally considered to be against public policy, and any group seeking them will have a very hard battle on its hands.

COMMUNICATIONS TO CLERGY. Under the common law, at least for the last several hundred years, communications to clergy or other church or ecclesiastical officers are not considered privileged, although judges have been reluctant to compel the disclosure of such communications. This rule applies unless it has been changed by statute. In the majority of states, however, the common-law rule has been changed by appropriate statutes. In substance, they provide that ministers of the gospel, rabbis, or priests of any denomination are incompetent to testify concerning communications made to them in their professional character, in the course of discipline enjoined by the rules or practice of their denomination. Such a statute has even been held applicable to confessions by a member of the Presbyterian Church when brought for discipline before the pastor and elders composing the church Session.

The tendency of the courts is toward a strict construction of those statutes making communications to clergy privileged, and, usually, only those communications are privileged which are made under the exact conditions enumerated in the statutes. It must definitely appear that the statements to the ministers, rabbis, or priests are made to them in their professional character, and in the course of discipline enjoined by the rules of practice of the denomination to which they belong. It has further been held that communications protected are limited to those that are penitential in their character or are made to clergy in obedience to some supposed religious duty or obligation.

In determining whether a communication is privileged, however, a court may not require the disclosure of a confession to clergy to determine whether it is privileged. The court must determine the question from the circumstances and facts leading up to the making of the confession. The disclosure should not be required unless it appears that the claim of privilege is being erroneously made.[15]

In chapter thirteen we will examine in detail the different statute provisions governing communications to clergy, along with significant cases by which these statutes have been interpreted.

Why Grant the Privilege to Clergy? On what basis has the law seen fit to grant the rights of privileged communications to the priest-penitent relationship? John Henry Wigmore, one of the greatest of recognized legal commentators, discusses the problem in his multi-volume *Treatise on the Anglo-American System of Evidence in Trials at Common Law.* While he regards it as an open question whether this privilege was recognized in common-law courts during the period before the Restoration, he concludes that since the Restoration it has been denied in the English courts. However, he also concludes that his four conditions of legitimate privilege exist in this case and the privilege should be recognized. These conditions are:

(1) The communications must originate in a *confidence* that they will not be disclosed;
(2) This element of *confidentiality must be essential* to the full and satisfactory maintenance of the relation between the parties;
(3) The *relation* must be one which in the opinion of the community ought to be sedulously *fostered;* and
(4) The *injury* that would inure to the relation by the disclosure of the communications must be *greater than the benefit* thereby gained for the correct disposal of litigation.[16]

These conditions and the arguments for them were advanced by Wigmore about 1905. In turn they influenced legislation to provide statutes on this privilege in a majority of the states of the Union. A glance at the Appendix, giving the date the statute guaranteeing the priest-penitent privilege was passed in these states, shows that most have been enacted since the publication of his arguments.

Who defines church, clergy, and ministry? One of the more troublesome questions on the current church-state scene has to do with who defines the nature and functions of religions and churches. What is church? Who is clergy? What is ministry? For there to be a recognizable separation between church and state, governments must be able to discern the difference between a church and some other kind of organization, between clergy and educators or therapists.

If there is to be some privilege accorded conversations held in confidence with clergy, then the courts need some way of knowing who comprises clergy. If the privilege hinges on some discipline enjoined by a church, then the courts need to know what is a church.

Up until 1969 there was a general but undefined accord among churches and governments in the United States about such definitions under the law. Attempts by government to specify the meanings proliferated, especially after Congress adopted major revisions to Section 6033 of the Internal Revenue Code.[17] In the past decade, the discussion has heated up considerably and is likely to remain warm through the decade ahead.

The Constitution of the United States does not contain the words *church, ministry,* or *clergy.* The word *religion* is found only once, in the First Amendment. The word *religious* is found only in Article VI.3 which prohibits a "religious Test . . . as a Qualification to any Office or public Trust under the United States."[18]

All of these words occur with much greater frequency in the constitutions and statutes of the states, most often in laws granting an exemption to various laws and regulations. With increasing frequency over the past decade they have appeared also in administrative rules and regulations of local, state, and federal agencies.

There are no definitions for clergy, church, or religion based in common law. When such matters were mentioned in statutes, it was assumed that those who needed to know what the words meant actually did know. So the question is now left to statutes, administrative regulations, and judicial review.

In the Mormon cases of the nineteenth century, the United States Supreme Court used the Christian religion as the norm and found that the Mormon practice of polygamy was not consistent with that norm.[19] Later, however, the court moved to other tests, including one of "common understanding." In striking down a Maryland law requiring public officials to take an oath affirming belief in the existence of God the court found that the word *religion* does not require such a belief but might include nontheistic understandings as well.[20] A number of state courts have followed this path, including within the meaning of religion all categories of belief that are commonly recognized as having religious roots—such systems as Ethical Culture and Transcendental Meditation.[21] A federal court in California found that the Universal Life Church, which ordains any applicant upon request by mail, is a religion in the sense of the First Amendment.[22]

By far the most administrative and legal activity in federal attempts to define the nature of churches, clergy, and religion has been in relation to the tax code. Congress has never enacted any definition of church or religious organization, but IRS has promulgated regulations which indicate that the critical test of whether an organization is a church or not rests primarily upon the conduct of religious worship.[23] An organization that does not conduct liturgical events recognizable as worship is not a church, even if it is clearly a function of a church or carries on functions that are clearly religious in character. This has possible implications for counseling services and other similar functions sponsored by a church.

The possible danger here is increased by regulations first proposed in 1976 in which IRS defined an "integrated auxiliary" of a church. This term had been introduced, and left undefined, by the Congress in the 1969 revisions of the tax code.[24] The IRS regulations said that the major purpose of integrated auxiliaries of churches must be "to carry out the tenants, functions and principles of faith of the church," and must "directly promote religious activities among the members of the church."[25] This specifically excluded

church-related hospitals, nursing homes, retirement centers, parochial schools, and, probably, counseling centers or
similar functions.

The proposed regulation brought a storm of protest from
American churches. The result was some changes in the
final regulation, but not enough change to clarify the
problems presented by the IRS rule. Promulgated in 1977,
the final regulations say that the "principal activity" of an
integrated auxiliary must be "exclusively religious," which
means that it cannot be primarily educational, charitable, or
any other nature than one which relates to the conduct of
strictly religious activities. Again, specifically excluded are
hospitals, orphanages, nursing homes, social service agencies, and, presumably, counseling services.

But who is clergy under the statutes granting privilege?
This varies from state to state. Most recent laws specify
"ministers, priests, rabbis, and Christian Science practitioners." From case law it is clear that a Catholic sister is not
clergy[26]; that elders and deacons of The Christian Church
are not ministers[27]; that ruling elders of the Presbyterian
Church sitting as the Session are "ministers of the Gospel"[28];
that non-ordained assistants to a minister, acting under his
or her direct supervision, may be subject to a claim of
privilege.[29]

Some states have included special qualifications in their
definitions. Kansas, for example, places the condition that
the minister "as his or her customary vocation preaches and
teaches the principles of religion and administers the
ordinances of his or her church, sect or organization."
Alabama extends coverage to "any duly ordained, licensed
or commissioned minister, pastor, priest, rabbi or practitioner of any bonafide established church or religious
organization . . . who regularly, as a vocation, devotes a
substantial portion of his time or abilities to the service of his
respective church or religious organization." Mississippi

extends the privilege to "a clergyman's secretary, stenographer or clerk." Oklahoma, North Dakota, Nebraska, and Wisconsin apply the privilege to a non-minister whom the person making the communication "reasonably believes to be" a minister at the time the communication is made.

In attempting to define clergy either directly or by limitation, state statutes may have created circumstances that can cause significant legal tangles upon litigation. For example, Pennsylvania would omit "clergymen or ministers who are self-ordained or who are members of religious organizations in which members other than the leader thereof are deemed clergymen or ministers." This would seem to rule out a finding in a Pennsylvania court like the Iowa ruling regarding Presbyterian ruling elders. It would also limit the rights of Jehovah's Witnesses, who consider all members to be ministers, as this statement makes clear:

> Jehovah's Witnesses constitute a society of ministers. . . . He has been "called" to the ministry by his fellow believers, and the Witnesses resent very deeply the fact that the persons whom they have called to the ministerial office are refused the recognition and denied the privileges that the Anglican parson, the Catholic priest, and the Methodist or Baptist or Congregational minister enjoy.[30]

Two states would impose an age limit on their definitions of clergy under the confidentiality statutes. Tennessee requires that the minister be over twenty-one years of age and Virginia says the minister must be over eighteen. Many denominations—Southern Baptists being the largest—have no such age requirements for ordinands.

Florida imposes a definitional limit upon which clerical orders of the Episcopal Church are covered by specifying a "rector of the Episcopal Church," when rectors are only one category of clergy in that church empowered to hear confessions under canon law—with bishops being the most obvious order excluded in Florida. Presumably, the Episcopal bishop of Florida and any other Episcopal clergy not in charge of a parish are excluded from the Florida law by its definitions. Bishops of the Roman Catholic Church and bishops in other denominations as well as non-parish clergy are apparently covered.

While a number of states impose limits, such as these, on their definitions, no state attempts to give an overall definition to the words *minister, priest, rabbi, clergy, church,* or *religious organization.* The churches have maintained historically that the state is not competent to make such definitions and that for the state to do so would constitute an "establishment" of those religious groups meeting the government's definitions and an "abridgment of the free exercise" of those not meeting them.

Chapter *XII*/COMMUNICATIONS TO CLERGY UNDER THE COMMON LAW

The commentators on the laws of evidence generally agree that after the Restoration, the common law recognized no right of privileged communications to clergy. Wigmore, in his definitive work on the Anglo-American system of evidence, says that while it is open to argument whether the privilege was recognized prior to the Restoration, the almost unanimous expression of judicial opinion since that time has denied the existence of the privilege as a rule of the common law.[1]

What this has actually meant is that where no statute existed, the common law has been interpreted more or less rigorously according to the historical situation of the time and the personal disposition of the ruling judge. This chapter will illustrate the wide variety of possible interpretations of the priest-penitent privilege where no statute exists.

The Case of Constance Kent. Let us begin by citing a rather interesting bit of correspondence concerning the case of Constance Kent. The details of her crime and trial are unimportant for us. Significant is the fact that her pastor, the Reverend A. D. Wagner, an Anglican priest, knew facts about her criminal act which had come to him in the course

of her confession to him as her spiritual advisor. The trial
took place near the end of the last century. What follows is
the opinion of two distinguished jurists on the question of
Mr. Wagner's testifying as a witness at the trial. Their
opposing points of view sharpen the issue for us.

In 1890, Lord Chief Justice Coleridge wrote a letter to
Mr. Gladstone (later prime minister of England) which
referred to the case of Constance Kent.

> I should not bore you, but I think perhaps it may interest you
> to know what Willes (Sir *James*) once told me he thought as to
> confession. He was, on the whole, the greatest and *largest*
> lawyer I ever knew, and I knew Jessel, Cairns and Campbell. I
> defended Constance Kent, John Karslake prosecuted her,
> and Willes tried her at Salisbury. Wagner was to have been a
> witness, and Willes had made up his mind that he should have
> to *hold* one way or the other as to the sanctity of confession. He
> took infinite pains to be right and he was much interested,
> because the point, since the Reformation, had never been
> decided. There were strong dicta of strong Judges—Lord
> Ellenborough, Lord Wynford and Alderson—that they would
> never allow Counsel to ask a clergyman the question. On the
> other hand, Hill, a great lawyer and good man, *but* a strong
> Ulster Protestant, had said there was no *legal* privilege in a
> clergyman. The thing did not come to a decision, for
> Constance Kent pleaded guilty; and Karslake told me he
> should never have thought of putting the question to Wagner
> [the clergyman]; and I had resolved *if* he did (but I knew he
> was a gentleman) that as an advocate I would not object, but
> use it in my speech. Willes, however, I suppose did not know
> us quite so well as we knew each other; and he had prepared
> himself to *uphold* my objection if I made it. He said he had
> satisfied himself that there was a *legal* privilege in a priest to
> withhold what passed in confession. Confession, he said, is
> made for the purpose of absolution. Absolution is a judicial
> act. The priest in absolving acts as a Judge, and no Judge is
> ever obliged to state his reasons for his judicial determination.
> This, you see, puts it on grounds of general law, and would be
> as applicable to Manton, Oliver Cromwell's chaplain, who,
> most certainly, heard confessions and absolved, as to the Pope

himself. Whether the English Judges would have upheld
Willes' *law* I own I doubt, but I thought it might interest you to
know the opinion, and the grounds of it, of so great a lawyer
and so really considerable a man. Practically, while Barristers
and Judges are gentlemen the question can never arise. I am
told it never *has* arisen in Ireland in the worst times.[2]

Without commenting on the curious bit of casuistry
involved here on the part of Mr. Willes, we can consider him
representative of the point of view that the priest should not
tell what he has learned through the confessional.

Taking the opposite point of view was Sir Harry Poland.
His biographer, Ernest Bowen-Rowlands, reports the
following incident:

I showed Sir Harry the following passage from a report of
certain proceedings in the House of Lords, and Lord
Westbury's statement therein, and he agreed that it not only
was a fitting illustration of his manner, but also a succinct
opinion on the much vexed question of "Should a clergyman
tell?"
In answering Lord Westmeath, who had drawn the
attention of the House to the refusal of the Reverend A. D.
Wagner to answer a question put to him by the Magistrates at
Trowbridge—in the case of Constance Kent [the "Road
Murder"]—on the ground that what he knew had been told to
him under the seal of the Confessional, he [Lord Westbury]
. . . said ". . . There can be no doubt that in a suit or criminal
proceedings a clergyman of the Church of England is not
privileged so as to decline to answer a question which is put to
him for the purpose of justice, on the ground that his answer
would reveal something that he has known in confession. He is
compelled to answer such a question, and the law of England
does not even extend the privilege of refusing to answer to
Roman Catholic clergymen in dealing with a person of their
own persuasion. There can be no doubt, therefore, that Mr.
Wagner was under an obligation to have answered the
question put to him if it had been insisted upon."[3]

These revealing insights into the points of view of two English jurists show the breadth of interpretation possible under the common law. England did not have then, nor does it have now, any statute protecting the confidence revealed to a pastor by an act of confession from a parishioner. As we shall see, the secret nature of these confessions has not always been respected by English and American judges.

Where the Priest Had to Tell. Let us look at some cases where a communication to a pastor or priest was ruled, directly or by implication, not privileged. The earliest on record since the Restoration is simply known as Anonymous (1693, England). Lord Chief Justice Holt declared that communications with an attorney or scrivener were privileged; "for he is counsel to man, with whom he will advise, if he be intrusted and educated in such way of practice; otherwise, of a gentleman, parson, etc."[4] The meaning of the last ambiguous phrase is that the privilege would not apply to a pastor.

BUTLER V. MOORE (1802, IRELAND). The heir of Lord Dunboyne attempted to prove that his ancestor, who had been a Catholic, joined the Anglican Church and later returned to the Catholic Church. Under the law then in effect, if Lord Dunboyne had rejoined the Catholic Church, he was incapable of making a will to divide his property. The heir desired a larger share than he had received in the will. A Roman Catholic priest was called to testify to the deceased's final religious affiliation. He was asked: "What religion did Lord Dunboyne profess at the time of his death?" He refused to answer on the ground of "confidential communications made to him in the exercise of his clerical functions." Mr. Justice Smith declined to recognize the privilege claimed by the witness. He was found in contempt of court and jailed.[5]

CHRISTIAN SMITH'S CASE (1817, NEW YORK). The charge was murder. The Reverend Peter J. Van Pelt, a Protestant minister, was called by the prosecution to testify to a confession made to him by the accused—"communicated to me as a minister of the gospel." When the defense counsel objected, Justice Van Ness, having been told by the minister that he himself had no objection to testifying, ruled that the confession was not privileged. He said: "There is a grave distinction, between auricular confessions made to a priest in the course of discipline, according to the canons of the church, and those made to a minister of the gospel in confidence, merely as a friend or advisor."

This case is particularly interesting since it is the first on record in this country of an actual distinction being made between the confessional of the Roman Catholic Church and penitential communications made to a Protestant pastor in his role as spiritual advisor to his flock.[6]

COMMONWEALTH V. DRAKE (1818, MASSACHUSETTS). The charge was lewdness. It was held that the defendant's penitential confessions to fellow members of his church were not privileged; therefore, their content was admitted as evidence.[7] The issue here was whether a public confession before a congregation had any claim of privilege. So far as this writer can determine, no court has ever held that it does. However, under statute law, in the case of Reutkemeier v. Nolte (1917, Iowa), to be considered later, a confession before the Session of a Presbyterian church was considered privileged, granting the Presbyterian ruling elder the same status before the law as the minister (the teaching elder).

REGINA V. HAY (1860, ENGLAND). In this case, referred to earlier in more detail, a Catholic priest objected to revealing the name of the person from whom he had received a watch charged as stolen. His claim was that he had received it in connection with the confessional. After continuing to refuse to answer the court's question, he was committed to jail by

Justice Hill for contempt of court, on the grounds that he was not asked to disclose anything *stated* to him in the confessional but only from whom he had received the watch.[8] Here we see the difficulty of establishing the broad limits of the penitential act and the danger of defining its scope too rigidly. Surely, the handing over of the watch by the thief to the priest was as much an act of privileged communication as any penitential words spoken. By it, guilt was acknowledged and confessed. At the same time we find here an implied recognition that the confession itself was a privileged communication. A footnote to the case points this up.

> It has been erroneously supposed that the learned Judge denied that any privilege attached to confession; but, as will be seen, he did not deny it; on the contrary, impliedly admitted it, and drew a distinction which would otherwise have been futile. That there is such a privilege can scarcely be denied. As a learned writer truly observes: "There cannot be a doubt that, previous to the Reformation, statements made to a priest under the seal of confession were privileged, except, perhaps, when the matter thus communicated amounted to high treason."[9]

NORMANSHAW V. NORMANSHAW (1893, ENGLAND). In this divorce case for the cause of adultery, the respondent had made certain admissions to the vicar, who was her pastor. The court "compelled" him to testify even though he claimed that the knowledge he had was privileged communication. In summing up, the president of the court said: "Each case of confidential communication should be dealt with on its own merits, but . . . it was not to be supposed for a single moment that a clergyman had any right to withhold information from a court of law."[10]

Where the Priest Was Silent. On the other hand, there are also a number of cases (not as many) decided on the basis of the common law where the pastor or priest was not required to testify to confidential communications made to him. For instance, in People v. Phillips (1813, New York), a priest was excused from testifying from whom he had received stolen goods. In this case, the court refused to follow the English cases and held that a Catholic priest was privileged from revealing the secrets of the confessional.[11] Two other instances are:

REGINA V. GRIFFIN (1853, ENGLAND). The chaplain of a workhouse was called as a witness to prove certain conversations with a prisoner. He stated that he had visited the accused "as her spiritual advisor to administer the consolations of religion." Baron Alderson held that he thought the conversations ought not to be given in evidence, on the ground that by analogy to the attorney's privilege, which secures "proper legal assistance" so the accused should have "proper spiritual assistance." The judge did add, however, "I do not lay this down as an absolute rule; but I think that such evidence ought not to be given." At this point the counsel for the prosecution stated that after such an intimation he would not tender the evidence.[12]

COOK V. CARROL (1945, IRELAND). A parish priest was called to testify concerning a statement made to him by one of his parishioners. The statement supposedly had some bearing on an investigation into the crime of seduction, of which the member was accused. The attorney for the prosecution contended that the priest was duty-bound to testify to what he knew so that the court could determine the guilt or innocence of the accused. The priest absolutely refused to testify on any matter which was brought to him in the course of confession. A question was raised whether the priest could be sentenced for contempt for refusing to offer the needed testimony. In this case, the Irish court pointed out that since the privilege was not recognized under the common law of England, the priest in England could be sentenced for refusing to cooperate with the court. But the judge went on to say that the common law of England is the common law of Ireland only to the extent that the English common law is not contrary to the national independence and the public policy of Ireland. The court then declared that the denial of the privilege of the confessional was a heresy which developed in the post-Reformation period and was contrary to the public policy of Ireland. The priest was not held in contempt for refusing to testify.[15]

This case will be referred to again when discussion centers on who holds the privilege—the priest or the penitent. In this trial the judge ruled that the privilege resides with the priest, and with him alone. For the time being, the case is significant because it is the only modern ruling under the common law where the priest-penitent privilege was granted and respected.

The difficulty that arises under the circumstances of such a decision is that it represents an exception to the rule rather than the rule. If this case indicated a contemporary understanding of the priest-penitent or pastor-parishioner privilege—an understanding that might bear considerable weight in any future rulings under common law—all might be well. But the very fact that this ruling was made in Ireland in favor of a Roman Catholic priest might prejudice a Protestant court in the United States to rule just the opposite. While the investigator feels that the judge ruled rightly in granting the communication the status of being privileged, so many other exceptional circumstances surround this ruling that it cannot be considered to be definitive for the future.

The Statement of Jeremy Bentham. One of the classic statements on the whole problem of privileged communications to clergymen was made quite a long time ago by Mr. Jeremy Bentham. Bentham, called by Wigmore the greatest opponent of privileges, did in the following argument concede that this privilege justified recognition.

> To form any comparative estimate of the bad and good effects flowing from this institution [the confessional], belongs not, even in a point of view purely temporal, to the design of this work. The basis of the inquiry is, that this institution is an essential feature of the catholic religion, and that the catholic religion is not to be suppressed by force . . . I set out with the supposition, that, in the country in question, the catholic religion was meant to be tolerated. But with any idea of toleration, a coercion of this nature is altogether inconsistent and incompatible. In the character of penitents, the people would be pressed with the whole weight of the penal branch of the law; inhibited from the exercise of this essential and indispensable article of their religion; prohibited, on pain of death, from the confession of all such misdeeds as, if judicially disclosed, would have the effect of drawing down upon them that punishment; and so, in the case of inferior misdeeds, combated by inferior punishments. Such would be the consequences to penitents; to confessors, the consequences would be at least equally oppressive. To them, it would be a downright persecution, if any hardship, inflicted on a man on a religious account, be susceptible of that, now happily odious, name. To all individuals of that profession, it would be an order to violate what by them is numbered amongst the most sacred of religious duties.[14]

This statement, a part of which has been quoted here, represents rather early thinking by a great legal mind which was certainly against the stream of opinion of that day. Bentham was a champion of Protestantism but based his argument on the guarantee of religious liberty which any faith ought to have. Since confession was a part of the discipline of the Roman Church, to be obeyed by all pious believers, he would have no part in undermining this article of their faith. While justice might at times suffer, the alternative he saw to be even worse, for it would amount to nothing less than religious persecution.

Mr. Bentham's opinion, expressed in 1827, was not always followed by later judges. Perhaps some were ignorant of it; others ignored it. The difficulty for us today is that it was stated on behalf of the sacramental context of the Roman Catholic confessional. Pastoral counseling in Protestantism today has no such sacramental dogma to support it. Its practice by pastor and people is not an article of faith in most Protestant denominations, although voluntary confession is officially encouraged by some. Would the argument about religious persecution apply to denial of privileged communication to Protestant pastors and people? I believe it would. There is no essential difference between a confession of sins made to a Roman Catholic priest and a confession made to a Protestant pastor. The required nature of one and the voluntary nature of the other is not definitive. In both, at their best, forgiveness is asked and absolution assured in the name of Jesus Christ, who alone has the power to forgive sins but who has given to men the ministry of reconciliation.

We may conclude that on the whole, privileged communication between priest and penitent has not fared well under the common law. While there are exceptions, such a privilege has not generally been recognized by the courts. If our concern is genuine in this cause to protect the penitential confidences between priest and penitent, whatever their faith, then we must work to establish such protection under statute law.

Chapter XIII/STATUTES ABOUT THE RIGHT TO SILENCE

Under what conditions has the priest-penitent privilege been granted by the statutes of various states in the United States? How have these statutes been interpreted by the courts? Let us begin by citing a typical statute, the one in effect in Minnesota at the time of the decision on the significant case, re Swenson (1931). The statute was passed by the legislature of the state in 1913. Its provisions are condensed here:

> Confession to clergyman, to be privileged, must be penitential in character and made to him in his professional character in confidence while seeking religious or spiritual advice, aid, or comfort; court, in determining whether confession to clergyman is privileged, cannot first require disclosure of confession; privileged character of confession to clergyman must be determined from surrounding facts and circumstances; disclosure of confession to clergyman should not be required unless it appears that claim to privilege is erroneously made.[1]

While the wording of the statutes of the various states differs somewhat, most contain about the provisions listed above. At the time of this writing, forty-nine states and several territories, plus some of the provinces of Canada, have similar statutes. (See Appendix.) In addition, the armed services in their court-martial provisions recognize the privilege.

The fact that a state has a statute on the priest-penitent privilege, however, does not guarantee that a minister may be excluded from testifying as a witness in a trial. In nearly all of the cases in which the statute has been invoked, the courts have recognized the rule, but have found that under the particular circumstances of the case it was not applicable. Although a privilege does exist in favor of not compelling clergy to testify concerning matters revealed to them in their professional character and in the course of church discipline, the statutes are strictly construed. Unless the facts surrounding the communication come squarely within the circumstances contemplated by the statute, the privilege will not be upheld.[2]

Statements Made to Clergy in Pursuance of Church Discipline. The courts have generally held or recognized that statements made to clergy in their professional character, and in the course of discipline enjoined by the rules or practice of the religious body to which they belong, are privileged communications.[3]

For instance, in Dehler v. State (1899, Indiana), the testimony offered by a Catholic priest was held to have been properly excluded, because the facts inquired of him were communicated to him as a confidential communication. The evidence showed that the communicant was a member of the Catholic Church, and that her conversation was with the priest as her pastor. The court stated that in view of other cases of this nature, confessions and admissions made to clergy in the course of discipline enjoined by their respective churches are inadmissible as evidence.[4]

The most significant case on this point is that of re Swenson. Emil Swenson, then pastor of Bethlehem Lutheran Church in Minneapolis, was brought before the Supreme Court of

Minnesota on appeal from the District Court of Hennepin County. He had been found guilty of contempt of court for refusing to answer certain questions put to him by the court in a divorce case. The basic facts were these:

Pastor Swenson had performed the marriage ceremony for the Sundseths, and both had been members of his church. Mr. Sundseth was a trustee of the church. One night Mr. Sundseth phoned Pastor Swenson and asked to see him. When he came to the parsonage and was ushered into the living room where other members of the family were seated, he said: "I want to see you in your private office." The two went upstairs to the pastor's study where they could be alone, and the door was closed. There Mr. Sundseth said to the minister, "I have something that I want to tell you and under the circumstances it is very hard for me to face my pastor." He then broke down in tears. The talk they had, according to Pastor Swenson, was confidential in origin and penitential in character. He testified that Sundseth discussed his intimate affairs with him at this interview, but he refused to disclose to the court what Mr. Sundseth had said to him. Mrs. Sundseth, in the meantime, had brought a divorce suit against her husband, on the grounds of adultery, and later sought to have the pastor called as a witness to substantiate her charge. He refused to answer the pertinent questions on the grounds that such statements as Sundseth made to him were made to him as a clergyman and that these communications were privileged.

The Supreme Court of Minnesota overruled the contempt conviction against Pastor Swenson by the District Court of Hennepin County. It did so on the basis of the following decision delivered by Chief Justice Wilson, of which part is here quoted:

> Under the common law, communications made to a minister of the gospel were not privileged. . . .

G. S. 1923, §9814, subd. 3, relating to privileged communications, reads: "A clergyman or other minister of any religion shall not, without the consent of the party making the confession, be allowed to disclose a confession made to him in his professional character, in the course of discipline enjoined by the rules or practice of the religious body to which he belongs."

Obviously the Legislature was not satisfied with the common-law rule. What then was the purpose in passing the statute? If we are to construe this statute as meaning that the only "confession" that is privileged is the compulsory one under the rules of the particular church, it would be applicable only, if our information is correct, to the priest of the Roman Catholic Church. Certainly the Legislature never intended the absurdity of having the protection extend to the clergy of but one church. . . . the statute says "clergyman or other minister of any religion," showing that the thought was to embrace the spiritual advisor of any religion whether he be termed priest, rabbi, clergyman, minister of the gospel, or any other official designation. It includes any one who may stand as a spiritual representative of his church. . . .

We are of the opinion that the "confession" contemplated by the statute has reference to a penitential acknowledgment to a clergyman of actual or supposed wrongdoing while seeking religious or spiritual advice, aid, or comfort, and that it applies to a voluntary "confession" as well as to one made under the mandate of the church. The clergyman's door should always be open; he should hear all who come regardless of their church affiliation. . . .

The statute has a direct reference to the church's "discipline" of and for the clergyman and as to his duties as enjoined by its rules or practice. It is a matter of common knowledge, and we take judicial notice of the fact, that such "discipline" is traditionally enjoined upon all clergymen by the practice of their respective churches. Under such "discipline" enjoined by such practice all faithful clergymen render such help to the spiritually sick and offer consolation to suppliants who come in response to the call of conscience. . . .

It is important that the communication be made in such spirit and within the course of "discipline," and it is sufficient whether such "discipline" enjoins the clergyman to receive the communication or whether it enjoins the other party, if a member of the church, to deliver the communication. Such practice makes the communication privileged, when accompanied by the essential characteristics, though made by a person not a member of the particular church or of any church. Man, regardless of his religious affiliation, whose conscience is shrunken and whose soul is puny, enters the clergyman's door in despair and gloom; he there finds consolation and hope. It is said that God through the clergy resuscitates. The clergymen practice the thought that "the finest of all altars is the soul of any unhappy man who is consoled and thanks God."[5]

Since this decision has been written, the courts have had little doubt that where the proper statute and confessional acts exist, penitential communications made to clergy of any denomination are privileged. This holds even when the confessant is not a member of the clergyman's church or of any church. Most decisions since the writing of the one above refer to it as their basic reference source.

Statements Made to Clergy Not in Pursuance of Church Discipline. It seems to be settled that statements made to clergy not in the course of discipline or similarly enjoined obligation by the church are not privileged.[6]

For instance, in Johnson v. Commonwealth (1949, Kentucky), a prosecution for willful murder, a pastor of the Methodist Church was introduced as a witness and testified that he visited the defendant in the county jail on the night of the day the deceased was shot. The defendant, in the course of his conversation with the pastor, stated that he had lost his temper and killed the deceased. An objection was made on the grounds that the statement was a privileged communication under statute. An examination of the evidence revealed, however, that there was nothing to indicate that the communication to the witness was penitential in its character or that it was made to the minister in his professional character or in the course of discipline enjoined by the rules of practice of his denomination. On the contrary, it did reveal that the visits of the pastor to the jail where the defendant was held were voluntary on his part and unsolicited, and that the statement in question was not made because of some religious duty. On the basis of this showing the court found that the communication was not privileged, and that there was no prejudicial error in allowing the pastor to testify concerning it.[7]

In another case, during the progress of a will contest a Methodist minister was permitted to testify that he had had conversations with the testator in which the latter spoke of his past life and of his adulterous relations with the beneficiary, his housekeeper, and of her great influence over him. On one of these occasions the testator had spoken penitently of his conduct and of a desire to join the minister's church, to which testimony the appellant objected on the ground that the communications were, by statute, privileged. In denying that such a privilege existed under the present circumstances, the court in Alford v. Johnson (1912, Arkansas) stated that the communications privileged by the statute were those made in the course of discipline by reason of the rules of the religious denomination. It was pointed out by the court that, from the testimony, it did not appear that the statements made by the testator to the minister were made to him in his professional capacity as a clergyman, nor was there any testimony that such statements were made in the course of discipline enjoined by any rules of practice of the religious denomination of which the testator was a member.[8] Many other cases of a similar nature have been decided the same way.

On the other hand, in one of the latest cases on record, Mullen v. United States (1958, District of Columbia), confessions made to a Lutheran minister by a person who was not a member of his church, but to whom he had promised spiritual aid if she confessed, were ruled privileged. Since this case has some significant aspects relating to our discussion, we will reproduce it in more detail than usual.

Carolyn Mullen, a mother, left her children chained in her home while she was absent. After having been tried in the United States District Court for the District of Columbia, she was convicted under a federal statute making it a crime to torture, beat cruelly, abuse, or otherwise willfully maltreat a child. On appeal, her case was heard by the United States Court of Appeals, District of Columbia Circuit, on November 21, 1958. A decision was handed down on December 4, 1958, in which the judgment of the lower court was reversed. One reason for the reversal was that the testimony by a Lutheran minister to the effect that the defendant had admitted to him that she had chained her children was privileged communication and should not have been allowed.

In a later written opinion, delivered on January 29, 1959, Circuit Judge Fahy wrote:

> When the case was decided December 4, 1958, I concurred and stated that I would later give my views on the question of admissibility of the testimony of a minister as to statements made to him by appellant as a penitent in preparation for receiving communion as a Lutheran communicant. The question is whether these statements were privileged communications . . . and, therefore, not admissible in evidence.
>
> The minister had testified briefly as a character witness for appellant. He then appears to have become troubled because of what occurred subsequent to his testimony. Appellant had taken the stand and had denied chaining the children. The minister then asked to see the trial judge and visited him in chambers, where he stated that he felt he had been unable to say all that his conscience impelled him to say. As a result the judge himself recalled the minister as the court's witness to give further evidence. After stating his impressions of the

family and the relations between the children and appellant, their mother, the minister testified as follows:

"After I had seen the defendant in the District Jail, she came to my office. She wanted to know whether she could come to communion. I advised her that as long as there was any suspicion as to her mistreating the children by chaining them I could not admit her to communion; that the Good Book says that if we confess our sins God is faithful and just to forgive us our sins and to cleanse us from all unrighteousness.

"She admitted that she had chained the children with the explanation that she did it for their protection. . . .

"I advised her and counselled with her that that was wrong and sinful." . . .

Was the disclosure of appellant to the minister a confidential confession to spiritual advisor? The answer would be clearer were the relationship of priest and penitent involved, where the priest is known to be bound to silence by the discipline and laws of his church. The present witness appears not to have felt bound in this manner. But I think the privilege if it exists includes a confession by a penitent to a minister in his capacity as such to obtain such spiritual aid as was sought and held out in this instance. (See Footnote: In re Swenson . . . where, though the statute applied to such a confession "in the course of discipline enjoined by the rules or practice of the religious body to which he [the minister] belongs"—in that case also the Lutheran Church—the privilege was recognized.) The minister definitely indicated that by confessing her sins to him appellant would receive the spiritual benefits she desired. In any event, enough was indicated to cause further inquiry by the court as to the character of the disclosure if doubt remained. In these circumstances I deem it appropriate to reach the question of admissibility, especially as the question might arise again should the case be retried. My view is that such a confession is a privileged communication which is not competent evidence on a trial, at least in the absence of the penitent's consent to its use.

The resolution of the problem today for federal courts is to be found in a proper application of Rule 26, Fed. R. Crim. P., adopted in 1948 under the authority of Congress. This Rule provides: ". . . The admissibility of evidence and the competency and privileges of witnesses shall be governed, except when an act of Congress or these rules otherwise provide, by the principles of the common law as they may be interpreted by the courts of the United States in the light of reason and experience."

The decisions to which we have referred [see source cited], as well as Rule 26, leave the federal courts, with ultimate authority in the Supreme Court, free to resolve our present question without additional legislation. It is true that the trend of decision has been chiefly in the direction of enlarging rather than restricting the area of admissibility of evidence, but the governing principle is the same. When reason and experience call for recognition of a privilege which has the effect of restricting evidence the dead hand of the common law will not restrain such recognition.

. . . In our own time, with its climate of religious freedom, there remains no barrier to adoption by the federal courts of a rule of evidence on this subject dictated by sound policy.

Sound policy—reason and experience—concedes to religious liberty a rule of evidence that a clergyman shall not disclose on a trial the secrets of a penitent's confidential confession to him, at least absent [of] the penitent's consent. Knowledge so acquired in the performance of a spiritual function as indicated in this case is not to be transformed into evidence to be given to the whole world. . . . The rules of evidence have always been concerned not only with truth but with the manner of its ascertainment.

Circuit Judge Edgerton, in commenting on this same final point, wrote: "As Mr. Justice Holmes said of wire-tapping, 'We have to choose, and for my part I think it a less evil that some criminals should escape than that the Government should play an ignoble part.'"[9]

This decision, even though made without a federal statute on the subject, seems to belong in our discussion of statute laws, because it is based on an interpretation of Rule 26, of the Federal Rules of Criminal Procedure. It amounts to the fact that the United States Court of Appeals has ruled the common law obsolete on the priest-penitent privilege and has proceeded, under Rule 26, to recognize it, even without a statute permitting it. This is, without doubt, a historic decision and will influence future decisions on cases where the priest-penitent privilege is called into question in the federal court system.

Statements Made by Clergy. The question has arisen several times as to whether the privilege associated with communications made to clergy should be extended to include communications made by clergy. In most cases, the courts have ruled that it does.

In Gill v. Bouchard (1896, Quebec), an action against a priest for wrongfully and illegally inducing an apprentice to leave the service of an employer, an attempt was made to distinguish between the element of privilege with regard to what the penitent said to his confessor and what the priest said in reply. The court upheld the objection of the priest to revealing anything that he might have said to the apprentice during the confession as being privileged and inadmissible. At the same time, however, the court made clear that the judgment was not based on the fact that the priest had taken an oath not to reveal such communications. Rather, the court stated that the privilege was founded entirely upon the provision of the Code, based upon grounds of public order, and was applicable to anyone discharging a religious office to whom a confidential statement was made by reason of that office.[10]

In another case, Ouellet v. Sicotte (1896, Quebec), a conversation had by a priest with the defendant under the seal of professional secrecy as his religious advisor was held privileged under a provision of the Quebec Code of Civil Procedure, that a witness cannot be compelled to declare what has been revealed to him confidentially in his professional character as religious advisor.[11]

However, in Bahrey v. Poniatishin (1920, New Jersey), an action against a priest for slander, a witness was asked to testify what the priest had said to her regarding the plaintiff, on an occasion when the witness was attending confession. In this case, the court held that there was no error in the admission of such testimony.[12]

Status of Person to Whom Statements Are Made. The courts have held that the privilege accorded to communications made to clergy does not apply to communications made to church officials or church members. The one exception to this rule seems to be the Presbyterian ruling elder.[13]

In Knight v. Lee (1881, Indiana), a slander action, Andrew Knight, the defendant, was visited by Robert C. Bryant, a Disciples of Christ elder and deacon, ". . . endeavoring to learn from the defendant what he knew, and what he would say in regard to the plaintiff's conduct and character." The plaintiff was a member of the same church as Mr. Bryant and had been up for church discipline. Mr. Bryant was a member of a church committee that had been officially appointed to look into charges against the plaintiff. The plaintiff later brought charges of slander against the defendant, Mr. Knight. When the defendant objected that his statements made to a member of the church committee were confidential communications within the meaning of a statute providing that clergymen should be incompetent to testify concerning confessions made to them in the course of discipline enjoined by their church, and therefore could not be repeated before the court, his objections were overruled. The basis for the court's decision was that the elder was not acting in the capacity of a clergyman at the time of the conversation and that the information imparted to him by the defendant was not a confession within the meaning of the statute.[14]

In People v. Gates (1835, New York), an objection was raised to the proof of certain admissions made by the defendant to the president of the consistory of the church.

The objection was based on the grounds that, in essence, they were confessions made to a clergyman. The charge was that the defendant, by false pretenses, had obtained the signature of the president to a bond and promissory note. Overruling the objection, the court based its action on the testimony of the president himself when he stated that he did not consider that the communications were made to him in his professional character or as a clergyman.[15]

The one instance where the courts have upheld as privileged certain penitential communications made to church officers is in the case of Reutkemeier v. Nolte, where these communications were made to ruling elders of a Presbyterian church. The case came, by appeal, to the Iowa Supreme Court, where, in 1917, Justice Evans delivered the opinion for the court.

> The facts as contended by plaintiff, briefly stated, are that in September, 1912, the defendant, a man then twenty-one years of age, had carnal knowledge of the plaintiff's daughter Mary, then a child only fourteen years of age. In June, 1913, she gave birth to a child alleged to be the result of such intercourse. The plaintiff was at the time a farmer, living upon his own farm. He was a widower with three daughters and three sons, all living with him at his home. . . .
>
> Plaintiff's daughter was a member of the Presbyterian Church. In the month of March before her child was born she was asked to appear, and did appear, before the church session. Such session consisted of the pastor and the three ruling elders. She appears to have confessed her sin and to have made certain communication to the elders. On the trial of this case the defendant sought to show what such communication was. It was claimed for the defendant that such communication involved others as well as himself, and that at least it cast much uncertainty upon the paternity of the child. The plaintiff objected . . .
>
> [The Code which governed the case was:] ". . . No practising attorney, counselor, physician, surgeon, or the stenographer or confidential clerk of any person, who obtains

such information by reason of his employment, minister of the Gospel or priest of any denomination shall be allowed, in giving testimony, to disclose any confidential communication properly intrusted to him in his professional capacity, and necessary and proper to enable him to discharge the functions of his office according to the usual course of practice or discipline. Such prohibition shall not apply to cases where the party in whose favor the same is made waives the rights conferred."

In applying this section to the case before us two questions naturally arise: (1) Was the communication a confidential one? (2) Were the recipients of such communication ministers of the Gospel within the meaning of the statute? As to the first question, it is apparent that the communication was of such a nature as would usually and naturally be deemed confidential, if for no other reason than that it involved a confession of sin to a spiritual advisor. We feel no hesitancy in holding the affirmative on this question. The second question presents greater difficulty. What is a "minister of the Gospel" within the meaning of this statute? The law as such sets up no standard or criterion. That question is left wholly to the recognition of the denomination. The word "minister," which in its original sense meant a mere servant, has grown in many directions and into much dignity. Few English words have a more varied meaning. In the religious world it is often, if not generally, used as referring to a pastor of the Church and a preacher of the Gospel. This meaning, however, is not applicable to all Christian denominations. Some of them have no pastors and recognize no one as a minister in that sense, and yet all denominations recognize the spiritual authority of the Church and provide a source of spiritual advice and discipline. The record herein contains a copy of the "Confession of Faith" of the Presbyterian Church, as well as other standard booklets setting forth the doctrine and policy [polity] of that denomination. The following excerpts therefrom will sufficiently indicate the same:

"That our blessed Saviour, for the edification of the visible Church which is his body, appointed officers, not only to preach the Gospel and administer the sacraments, but also to exercise discipline, for the preservation both of truth and duty; and that it is incumbent upon these officers, and upon the whole Church, in whose name they act, to censure or cast out the erroneous and scandalous, observing in all cases the rules contained in the Word of God."

"The ordinary and perpetual officers in the Church are bishops or pastors; the representatives of the people, usually styled ruling elders; and deacons." . . .

"Ruling elders are properly the representatives of the people chosen by them for the purpose of exercising government and discipline, in conjunction with pastors or ministers. This office has been understood by a great part of the Protestant Reformed Churches to be designated in the Holy Scriptures by the title of governments, and of those who rule well, but do not labor in the Word and doctrine."

"1. The church session consists of the pastor or pastors and ruling elders, of a particular congregation." . . .

"6. The church session is charged with maintaining the spiritual government of the congregation, for which purpose they have power to inquire into the knowledge and Christian conduct of the members of the church; to call before them offenders and witnesses, being members of their own congregation, and to introduce other witnesses where it may be necessary to bring the process to issue, and when they can be procured to attend; to receive members into the Church; to admonish, to rebuke, to suspend or exclude from the sacraments those who are found to deserve censure; to concert the best measures for promoting the spiritual interests of the congregation, to supervise the Sabbath school, and the various societies or agencies of the congregation; and to appoint delegates to the higher judicatories of the Church."

"To these officers the keys of the kingdom of heaven are committed, by virtue thereof they have power respectively to retain and remit sins, to shut that kingdom against the impenitent, both by the word and censures; and to open it unto penitent sinners, by the ministry of the Gospel, and by absolution from censures, as occasion shall require."

To the foregoing it may be added that the office of ruling elder is perpetual, and no person can be divested of it except by removal. These ruling elders have nothing to do with the temporal affairs of the Church, but deal wholly with its spiritual side and its discipline. It will be noted also, from what we have quoted, that, although it is required that the pastor of the congregation shall always be the moderator of the session, when there is a pastor, yet if there be no pastor and it be impracticable to obtain another pastor, the ruling elders are authorized to conduct the session without one. It will be noted also that there is no power of discipline conferred upon the pastor, except in conjunction with the ruling elders. The pastor of the Church is not denominated as a "minister," but as an elder or presbyter. The power of discipline conferred upon the pastor is conferred upon him only in a joint sense as one of the "officers." "These officers" are recognized as having power "to shut that kingdom against the impenitent both by the word and censures; and to open it unto penitent sinners, by the ministry of the Gospel, and by absolution from censures, as occasion shall require." . . .

The only course of discipline known to the Presbyterian denomination is that exercised by the ruling elders sitting jointly with the pastor as a moderator. The denomination itself by its Confession of Faith characterizes the work of these elders as a "ministry of the Gospel." The purpose of the statute is one of large public policy. We are told of one in an olden time who "found no place of repentance, though he sought it carefully with tears." This statute is based in part upon the idea that the human being does sometimes have need of a place of penitence and confession and spiritual discipline. When any person enters that secret chamber, this statute closes the door upon him, and civil authority turns away its ear. The privilege of the statute purports to be applicable to every Christian denomination of whatever polity. Under the polity of the Presbyterian denomination this privilege cannot be applicable to it, unless it be true that the ruling elders are "ministers of the Gospel" within the meaning of the statute. We find that they are such within the contemplation of the Presbyterian Confession of Faith, and therefore that they are such within the meaning of the statute. We hold that the trial court ruled correctly at this point.[16]

This ruling is most significant for the reason that the statute on privileged communication is broadened to include the constitutionally constituted disciplinary body of the Presbyterian Church—its Session. The court acknowledged that in the Presbyterian Church the Session stands in much the same disciplinary relationship to the members of the congregation as the priest alone does in the Roman Catholic Church. Whether this ruling would apply to other denominations having ordained officers charged with the spiritual discipline of the congregation is not known. But logic would seem to point that way.

Statements Involving Third Persons. In those cases in which the communication sought to be declared privileged involved a third person, the courts have held that it was not. This has been the decision whether that communication related to the act of a third person or was made for the purpose of being transmitted to a third person.[17]

First, consider those communications relating to the *act* of a third person. In Commonwealth v. Gallo (1931, Massachusetts), it was shown, during a trial for murder, that the defendant had made statements regarding the fact that his co-defendant was implicated in the crime. In the closing argument of both the defense attorney and the district attorney, reference was made to the fact that one of those to whom the defendant had made the statements was the priest at the state prison. Exceptions were later taken to the argument of each of these attorneys. The court held that the trial judge had properly instructed the jury that reference to the statements of the defendant as a confession or preparation for death was going too far and should be disregarded; the court further held that in a proper way the statements were subject to comment in argument.[18]

And in Christensen v. Pestorious (1933, Minnesota), a trial for the wrongful death of a woman, a passenger in an automobile that had collided with a train, a pastor was called as a witness to state what the defendant's daughter, also a passenger in the automobile, had said to him about the accident. The defendant contended that the woman had said nothing by way of warning or otherwise as the car approached the railroad crossing or at the time of the collision. She, therefore, was negligent in failing to warn the defendant so as to avert the accident. During the trial the daughter of the defendant stated that the woman had said nothing by way of warning or otherwise. However, her pastor testified that when he called on the daughter in the hospital after the accident, she had said to him that the woman had called out the words, "the train," just at the time of the accident. The defendant objected to the testimony on the ground that it involved a privileged communication. The court found, however, that while the pastor had called upon the witness at the hospital prepared to give spiritual advice and comfort if the occasion required, it was beyond controversy that he had received nothing but an ordinary description of the occurrence. Under the circumstances, this could not be deemed privileged.[19]

In the cases where the communication was to be *transmitted to* a third person, the courts have also held that it was not privileged. In Hills v. State (1901, Nebraska), the defendant, almost immediately after his arrest on a charge of bigamy, sent for a minister. He asked the clergyman to intercede with his first wife for a settlement of the criminal proceedings, writing out a synopsis of what he wanted the minister to say. The minister was later called to testify about the contents of this communication, and an objection was raised. The court held that according to the statute, to render a communication to a minister of the gospel or priest privileged, it must have been received in confidence, and with the understanding, express or implied, that it should not be revealed to anyone. Since this communication had been made for the express purpose of being transmitted to a third person, the necessary element of secrecy was not present and the communication could not be regarded as confidential.[20]

In Mitsunaga v. People (1913, Colorado), the defendant,

in jail on a murder charge, was visited by a minister. The prisoner sent word by the minister to the chief of police that he wished to make a statement concerning his association with the crime. When he was taken to the chief, the defendant, through interpreters, made two statements. During the trial he claimed that they were privileged, made to the minister as a spiritual advisor. The court held, however, that since the defendant had voluntarily employed the minister as an intermediary between himself and the chief of police, and then voluntarily made the statements, without having been influenced by any duress or coercion of any sort, there was no error in admitting the statements as evidence.[21]

One other situation arises under this category. What about privileged communications *overheard* by a third person? The courts have generally held that when a privileged communication is overheard, whether by accident or design, by some person not a member of the privileged relation or a necessary intermediary, such a person may testify as to the communication. In fact, that person is said to be absolutely unaffected by the rule of privilege. For instance, a third person who overhears a communication between husband and wife, attorney and client, or physician and patient, may give testimony about it. Most likely, although the situation has not arisen in the courts, if a person overhears a privileged communication between a minister and a penitent, that person would be allowed to give testimony about it. In every case the spying or eavesdropping nature of the overheard conversation may affect its weight as evidence but the content of the conversation would still be admissible.[22] This is one place where the author feels the law is wrong and at conflict with itself. If the law recognizes the existence of a privileged communication, its accidental or purposeful hearing by a third person does not change the nature of the privileged relationship. To be true to the spirit of the law recognizing privileged communications as well as the letter, a person ought not be allowed to testify about the communication simply because he or she may have overheard it.

Matters Communicated Otherwise Than by Oral Statements. On several occasions the courts have been called on to decide whether a privilege existed regarding information obtained by clergy through means other than by oral communications. Usually, the courts have held that it did not, although there seem to be exceptions.

In Schaeffer's Estate (1941, Pennsylvania), a minister was called to testify as a witness about his efforts to effect a reconciliation between a husband and a wife. This was objected to on the ground that it constituted a confidential communication. Although the court overruled the objection principally on the ground that it did not relate to statements which were penitential in character and made to the minister in his professional character while seeking spiritual advice, the court also commented on the fact that some of the testimony was not based on communications of any sort but on personal observations.[23]

However, in Boyles v. Cora (1942, Iowa), a statute providing that a minister of the gospel or priest of any denomination should not be allowed, in giving testimony, to disclose any confidential communication made to him in his professional capacity was construed to include observations as well as communications.[24]

The significant case on this point seems to be that of Buuck v. Kruckeberg, the decision being made by the Indiana Appellate Court after hearing the case on December 7, 1950. The general facts about the case are these: The plaintiff brought suit for the division of real estate based on a deed from the defendant's mother and joint tenant. The defendant counterclaimed that the deed should be canceled on the grounds that it was procured by undue influence and that his mother was of unsound mind when she executed it. During the trial, the opinion testimony of a minister, intimately acquainted with the deceased, as to whether the defendant's mother was of sound mind at the time of the execution of the deed, was excluded on the grounds that this was privileged communication. The lower court found the deed valid and decreed partition of the real estate. The defendant appealed.

The Appellate Court of Indiana, in an opinion by Justice Crumpacker, reversed the lower court's judgment and remanded the case for a new trial. The grounds for the reversal were that the issues of undue influence and mental competency were questions of fact and that the exclusion of the clergyman's opinion testimony constituted prejudicial error. What follows is quoted from part of the judge's decision:

> During the course of the trial the appellant called one William L. Hofius as a witness. He testified that he is a minister and institutional chaplain of the Lutheran Church and as such has been conducting religious services and administering to the spiritual needs of institutional patients in Fort Wayne since 1941. During 1943 he made regular calls upon a member of the Lutheran Church who was confined in Carrie Blume's nursing home and thereby became well acquainted with her. In 1944 she asked him to conduct a service there, consisting of a short message and a prayer, which he did and has been doing regularly ever since on each Thursday morning. Necessarily his contacts with Mrs. Blume were frequent and in 1946 he observed an emotional change in her. Her feeling toward the appellant, whom she had theretofore considered an ideal son and praised constantly, completely reversed itself and she never spoke of or referred to him unless compelled to do so by the nature of the conversation. He was the subject of violent tirades on her part and she quieted down only when he, the witness, spoke to her in German of her early childhood training. On this testimony the witness was asked to express

his opinion as to the soundness of mind of Carrie Blume on the 31st day of January, 1947. The appellee objected to the question and upon the objection being sustained moved to strike out the entire testimony of the witness which motion was also sustained.

These rulings were made upon the theory that the testimony of the witness concerned matters communicated to him as a clergyman as to which he is made an incompetent witness by Burns' Statute §2-1714. The statute, however, made the witness incompetent only as to "confessions or admissions" made to him "in course of discipline enjoined by" his church. It is apparent that the testimony of Rev. Hofius concerned neither a confession nor an admission on the part of Carrie Blume made to him in the course of any disciplinary action enjoined upon him by his church. He was clearly a competent witness and it was error to strike out his testimony and to refuse to receive his opinion based thereon as to Carrie Blume's soundness of mind.[25]

What about testimony concerning letters, handwriting, etc.? Can a minister be called to witness to these things? It appears that she or he can. In Colbert v. State, a prosecution for arson, the priest of the village where the fire occurred later received an anonymous letter purporting to be a confession by a man then in a hospital in another city. The letter stated that the gentleman in question had been a suitor of the defendant, but that she had rejected him, and that in revenge he deliberately set fire to the building burned after he saw her leave it. The priest took the letter to the defendant's residence and read it to her. He testified that she was excited and wrote at his dictation, and gave him a statement that no stranger spoke to her on the date of the fire, that she had no idea how the fire started, and that the letter was unknown to her. She even requested the priest to publish the letter. However, the priest testified that the handwriting of the original letter and of the statement written by the girl were the same. This conversation of the priest with the defendant was held not to be privileged under a statute forbidding the disclosure by a clergyman of a confession made to him in his professional character, because it was not a confession, and, further, because he was not acting in his professional character at the time.[26]

Who, Really, Possesses the Privilege? The courts seem to be almost unanimous in agreeing that the possessor of the privilege in the confidential communication between priest and penitent is the penitent. Nearly all the statutes are worded in such a way that the clergy cannot testify to the communication without the permission of the penitent. This, by elimination, gives the privilege, ultimately, to the penitent.

As we have seen earlier, Roman Catholic canon law places the privilege with the penitent, thereby forbidding the priest, or any third party who might have overheard the confession, from revealing the contents of the confessional without the permission of the confessant.

However, one case has reversed this historic acceptance of the privilege residing with the penitent. Decided on the basis of common law, it is the case of Cook v. Carrol, decided on July 31, 1945, at Dublin, but heard originally by the High Court on Circuit at Tralee, Judge Gavan Duffy presiding. A parish priest, the Reverend W. J. Behan, interviewed together in his house a girl parishioner who alleged that she had been seduced and the parishioner whom she held responsible for the act. Later, the girl's mother brought an action for damages against this parishioner, and the priest was called to give evidence of what passed at this interview. He refused to give evidence, claiming the communication was privileged. The Circuit Court at Listowel, where the case was first tried, found the priest in contempt and he was fined ten pounds. He did not appeal.

However, the plaintiff did, and again the priest was called

as a witness when the case was heard before the High Court. He again refused to answer on the grounds of privilege. In this instance, the contempt judgment of the lower court was reversed. Complicating the case was that in both instances, the girl and the man involved both testified as to what was said at the priest's house on the first interview. Their stories did not tally. Despite this, the priest still refused to testify, claiming the communication was privileged. The High Court not only held that the communication was privileged but that such privilege cannot be waived by a party thereto without the consent of the priest.

In discussing this point, Judge Duffy wrote:

> . . . one marked distinction merits notice. As between himself and his attorney, the client is master of the situation, so that if he thinks fit to waive his privilege, the privilege disappears and the lawyer, his paid servant, cannot set it up. But the priest is not hired, and a parishioner's waiver of privilege should not, as a matter of course, destroy the priest's right to keep his secret, where the sacerdotal privilege is regulated by law; I am speaking here of confidences outside the confessional, for, as Catholics know, the inviolable secrecy of the sacrament of penance stands alone and unique. . . .
>
> . . . to protect the priest against having to testify is only a half-measure of justice, if others may blurt out the conversation; the essential foundation of the relation established is the acceptance from the outset by all concerned of the inviolable secrecy of the meeting under the aegis of the parish priest; that is the capital consideration, and we must protect confidences which would never have been exchanged at all but for the absolute and implicit faith of his two parishioners in him. If in a crisis his extraordinary prestige as parish priest is utilized, we cannot afterwards, having got his aid in the closest secrecy, treat him as a cipher, a mere onlooker, whose determination to have the secret guarded may be ignored as soon as one of the contestants seeks to get the better of the other by broadcasting it.
>
> This is not at all the ordinary case of negotiations without prejudice between two adverse parties, who may agree to

waive a privilege which belongs to them alone. In a case of this
kind I think no publication whatever of the secret conversation is allowable, without the express permission of the parish
priest, though we know that he will almost invariably refuse it.
If, in an instance of this kind, we deny the tripartite character
of this privilege, we do an injustice to the priest, who has a real
and distinct interest as the parish priest in maintaining the
compact of secrecy. As I understand the tacit, but clear,
understanding of the three persons meeting under his roof,
simple good faith should be held to prevent two of them from
publishing anything there said, without the express prior
consent of the parish priest.

My main decision stands . . . I hold that the parish priest of
Ballybunion committed no contempt of the High Court on
Circuit.[27]

This decision should not be misinterpreted. In this case, the
court seems to have been caught in a dilemma caused by the
usual assumption that the privilege belongs to the penitent
and that he may waive it if he wishes. These penitents, if we
may call them that, did, but the priest out of honor and
obedience to what he conceived his sacred vows to include, still
chose not to testify. He was within his rights and the High
Court upheld these rights. But the one weakness of giving the
privilege to the penitent alone was exposed. Privileged
communication is always two-way communication. Each party
to the communication bears mutual responsibility to the other
for what passes between them. To give the privilege solely to
the penitent may, as in this instance, be grossly unfair and not
serve the public interest.

On the other hand, the conclusion reached by Judge
Duffy that the privilege, in this exceptional case, resides
with the priest alone is equally untenable. It also denies the
mutual responsibility that exists in such a relationship. If
applied in other situations, it could restrict the freedom
under the law which a penitent should retain. The author is
quite in agreement with the judge that in this case the

penitents should not have been allowed by the court to testify without the consent of the priest. The circumstances warrant this course of action. But to make any generalization from this instance that the privilege belongs to the priest alone is a dangerous precedent.

The privilege, it would seem, belongs to both parties and they are mutually responsible for preserving it. Neither party in a privileged communication should be allowed to testify to the contents of that communication without the consent of the other party. Furthermore, either party should retain the right not to testify to the contents of that communication even though the other party has given permission. This is the only way that both mutual responsibility for the contents of the communication and mutual respect for the freedom of the other person can be effected in this kind of situation. No rules can be laid down for determining in every case when a party to a privileged communication should give the other party the right to testify to it. Nor can any rules be projected, which would always apply, to guide either party on when to remain silent, even though he or she has the permission of the other party to testify. These decisions must be made on the basis of the circumstances of each case and our responsibilities in that situation. But so long as the law recognizes that the privilege belongs only to one or the other party, situations will continue to arise where injustice can happen and the public interest not be served.

The Current Situation. In 1942 the American Law Institute, meeting in Philadelphia, adopted its *Model Code of Evidence*. Rule 219 was entitled: "Priest-Penitent Privilege; Definition; Penitential Communications." It read:

(1) As used in this Rule,
    (a) "priest" means a priest, clergyman, minister of the gospel or other officer of a church or of a religious

denomination or organization, who in the course of its discipline or practice is authorized or accustomed to hear, and has a duty to keep secret, penitential communications made by members of his church, denomination or organization;

(b) "penitent" means a member of a church or religious denomination or organization who has made a penitential communication to a priest thereof;

(c) "penitential communication" means a confession of culpable conduct made secretly and in confidence by a penitent to a priest in the course of the discipline or practice of the church or religious denomination or organization of which the penitent is a member.

(2) A person, whether or not a party, has a privilege to refuse to disclose, and to prevent a witness from disclosing, a communication if he claims the privilege and the judge finds that

(a) the communication was a penitential communication, and

(b) the witness is the penitent or the priest, and

(c) the claimant is the penitent, or the priest making the claim on behalf of an absent penitent.[28]

Rule 219 had much to commend it. Its definition of priest and penitent are clear, concise, and inclusive of most imaginable relationships. It protects both the priest and penitent equally, although the privilege is seen as belonging to the penitent. There are no exceptions listed, such as a communication of treasonable conduct. In addition, it provides immunity for a person other than a minister in hearing a confession. However, it does not protect those communications made to a minister in confidence which might not be of a penitential character.

Originally, this rule had also been adopted in 1953 by the commissioners developing the *Uniform Rules of Evidence*. However, in 1974, the National Conference of Commissioners on Uniform State Laws developed a much broader statement for the new Uniform Rules. It reads as follows:

Rule 505. [Religious Privilege]
  (a) Definitions. As used in this rule:
    (1) A "clergyman" is a minister, priest, rabbi, accredited Christian Science Practitioner, or other similar functionary of a religious organization, or an individual reasonably believed so to be by the person consulting him.
    (2) A communication is "confidential" if made privately and not intended for further disclosure except to other persons present in furtherance of the purpose of the communication.
  (b) General rule of privilege. A person has a privilege to refuse to disclose and to prevent another from disclosing a confidential communication by the person to a clergyman in his professional character as spiritual advisor.
  (c) Who may claim the privilege. The privilege may be claimed by the person, by his guardian or conservator, or by his personal representative if he is deceased. The person who was the clergyman at the time of the communication is presumed to have authority to claim the privilege but only on behalf of the communicant.[29]

Notice here that the terms *priest, penitent,* and *penitential communication* have been done away with, and the whole rule set in the context of a situation descriptive of ordinary pastoral counseling.

Earlier, in 1972, the Supreme Court, in developing the new Federal Rules of Evidence, used almost identical words in its newly stated Rule 506. Only the last sentence was different. The Supreme Court substituted these words: "The clergyman may claim the privilege on behalf of the person. His authority so to do is presumed in the absence of evidence to the contrary."[30]

In all, the Supreme Court submitted to Congress thirteen rules defining privilege. In one comprehensive action, Congress impounded all thirteen and approved only General Rule 501, which reads:

"Except as otherwise required by the Constitution of the United States or provided by Act of Congress or in rules prescribed by the Supreme Court pursuant to statutory authority, the privilege of a witness, person, government, State, or political subdivision thereof shall be governed by the principles of the common law as they may be interpreted by the courts of the United States in the light of reason and experience. However, in civil actions and proceedings, with respect to an element of a claim or defense as to which State law supplies the rule of decision, the privilege of a witness, person, government, State, or political subdivision thereof shall be determined in accordance with State law."[31]

In rejecting all the Supreme Court's specific rules on privilege, the Congress left the law of privileges in its current condition to be developed by the courts utilizing the principles of the common law. It was not the intention of Congress to disapprove of the enumerated privileges or to freeze the law in its present state; rather, the action was intended to provide the courts with flexibility to develop rules of privilege on a case-by-case basis, modifying or eliminating some and recognizing new ones.

However, the privileges put forth by the Supreme Court remain as standards of considerable utility and will surely be taken seriously by the courts for years to come. We may, therefore, rejoice in this new openness to privilege by the federal courts and expect that those religious persons claiming privileges will be looked upon with some degree of sympathy by the courts. The courts of the states, however, are an entirely different matter, and there the state statutes will continue to apply. If any religious group within a state is unhappy with that state's laws, it must work from within the legislature to have those laws modified or changed.

Chapter XIV /
SPECIALIZED CLERGY: SPECIALIZED PROBLEMS

Most of what is said in this book deals with the clergy in relationship to parish or congregational responsibilities. Increasingly, however, the role of the minister is being expressed through other specialized forms. Many of these specialized ministries involve questions of privileged communications in ways that are at least as direct and crucial as those faced by a pastor. Among such areas of ministry are pastoral counseling, military and institutional chaplaincy, and family therapy.

Pastoral Counselors. Pastoral counselors are, usually, ordained clergy engaged in a special form of ministry for which they are prepared through an educational process grounded in theology and oriented toward pastoral care for persons and families. As such, they represent a particular and growing expression of a rich educational and theological heritage. Their perspectives draw heavily on the behavioral sciences to enlighten their understandings of human personality and human relationships. This perspective is one set of factors shaping and forming their function as ministers.

While their roots are planted in the historical soil of the religious community and its theological insights, they are also related to the life and behavioral sciences. It is this "secular" connection that implies both the strength and the weakness of the case for extension of the privilege to pastoral counselors.

For our purposes it is important to note the different contexts within which pastoral counselors undertake to provide their services to others. The growth of pastoral counseling centers apart from the parish or congregational setting is a phenomenon that has raised questions, many of them unresolved, about the nature of the counseling ministry. In that context is the counselor providing a legitimate function of ministry or has the bridge been crossed from clergy to mental health practitioner?

Unfortunately, many professional pastoral counselors seem to want it both ways. They want to be accepted as a behavioral scientist on the one hand, but want the benefits of a relationship to the religious community on the other. This situation clouds the public perception of the ordained person functioning in that setting, and probably jeopardizes the protection offered by the statutes of the states dealing with clergy confidentiality. In general, the protections provided to mental health practitioners are not nearly as broad as those provided for clergy.

Standards set by the several church-related professional and certification groups—American Association of Pastoral Counselors and Association for Clinical Pastoral Education— can help define and resolve some of the problems posed. There is little case law to guide a discussion of how the privilege applies to persons engaged in such a ministry.

Only New Hampshire has specifically provided for extension of the privilege to pastoral counselors, and the price for that protection is licensing by a state agency. (The District of Columbia law covers clergy "regarding efforts to reconcile estranged spouses"; the Iowa confidentiality statute applies to "counselors" as well as to "clergy"; Ohio covers "information confidentially communicated to him for a religious counseling purpose in his professional character.") New Hampshire instigated a furor among pastoral care professionals generally when it became the first state to regulate pastoral counselors as a part of its licensing procedures for mental health practitioners. While the state does not require all pastoral counselors to be licensed, the statute extends the protection of the privilege only to those who are licensed by the state.

Actually, New Hampshire has two privileged communications statutes that affect clergy. One is a general and quite limited traditional law.[1] The other relates specifically to pastoral counselors "licensed under this chapter," and places them under the much firmer protection similar to that "provided by law between attorney and client."[2]

The Ohio statute alluded to above was passed in 1980 and mentions "religious counseling" within the context of the privilege. Whether the courts would recognize this reference in regard to pastoral counseling as a discipline is a matter of speculation. A related Ohio statute was also revised in 1980, stipulating that those "providing counseling services to victims of crimes" are protected by a privilege.[3] This law defines "counseling services" to "include services provided in an informal setting by a person who, by education or experience, is competent to provide such services." Does this have the effect of extending coverage to pastoral counselors under certain circumstances?

Several states have laws to protect those involvements by clergy in the resolution of marital difficulties. Alabama, for example, covers communications with clergy "(3) to enlist help or advice in connection with a marital problem," and specifically extends the privilege both to the persons seeking help and to the clergy. The District of Columbia and Delaware have identical provisions protecting clergy "with respect to any communication made to him in his

professional capacity, by either spouse, in connection with
any effort to reconcile estranged spouses, without the
consent of the spouse making the communication."

In six other states—Iowa, Kentucky, Massachusetts,
Minnesota, North Carolina, and Tennessee—there is
somewhat nebulous language, different in each statute,
which seems to indicate that pastoral counselors who are
ordained clergy might be protected.

It should be noted that there is a case, however, in which a
California judge ruled that the privilege did not apply to a
religious or spiritual advisor acting as a marriage counselor.[4]

Thus far we have considered the problem associated with
pastoral counselors functioning in a center not directly
associated with the ministry of a particular church or
congregation. The second major context is directly within
the life of a religious community and is a part of its direct
ministry to its members and community.

When the ordained clergy-counselor functions in this
context it is likely that the problems regarding the privilege
are probably fewer, though there is no case law upon which
to base such an observation. Counseling services to
individuals, couples, and families in trouble are part of what
most clergy have always done. The fact that some clergy now
specialize in this field of ministry would not seem to change
the scope of protection, providing that some deliberate
decisions and actions are taken in advance.

One factor needing special attention has to do with fees
charged for services. While none of the statutes refer to how
a fee system might affect the relationship, some observers
believe that fees for counseling might represent to the
courts a clear demarkation between the provision of a
pastoral act protected by law and a commercial exchange
like that engaged in by other mental health practitioners.[5]

A second factor is a clear definition of the nature of the

counseling service approved by an authoritative action of the appropriate governing body of the church, stating that the counseling ministry is an actual part of the pastoral work of the church. One church judicatory, Hanover Presbytery of the Presbyterian Church in the U.S.A., has adopted guidelines for the specialized ministry of pastoral care, giving the Presbytery Commission on the Minister direct oversight of all its clergy engaged in this kind of work.

If proper care is taken to preserve the specifically religious nature of the counseling work as an actual part of the ministry of the church, it seems likely that a clergy member of a church staff engaged in pastoral care and counseling probably has the same protection afforded any other minister, priest, or rabbi in any given state.

Therapists Who Are Also Clergy. Clergy who work in secular settings as professional mental health practitioners or therapists present acute problems to the principle of clergy-penitent confidentiality. Such persons must be certain of their role definition, and of their self-definition, in order to be clear with themselves and their clients about the status of privileged communications.

In most states clergy enjoy broader protections than most mental health practitioners. Even psychiatrists (and other physicians, for that matter) do not have the scope of protection provided by some statutes to communications with clergy. Several years ago a California psychiatrist sought to test this differential by refusing to reveal information required by a court and then claiming in a suit that psychotherapists were being denied equal protection under the law in violation of the Fourteenth Amendment to the U.S. Constitution.[6] The court sidestepped the difficult constitutional question, but did find a distinction between the "religious conviction out of which the penitential privilege flows" and the relationship between a therapist and patient.

The once-proposed Federal Rules of Evidence did contain a psychotherapist-patient privilege, though its definitions of covered psychotherapists were quite narrow. Of course, the FRE was not adopted though it has continued to exercise considerable influence over considerations relating to the privilege.

Among the unknown factors affecting the therapist/ clergy practitioner is which role the courts would recognize. It seems most likely to this writer that the courts would ordinarily find that the therapist role weighs more heavily than the clergy role. This observation is based upon the precedent established in Simrin v. Simrin (cited earlier and detailed in chapter 9). In addition, in a case dealing with the dual roles of a military chaplain, who serves as both staff officer and spiritual advisor, the courts ruled that the former role predominated.[7]

Further, the trend is for courts to extend the privilege conservatively, since it is the view of most judges that the courts are entitled to "every man's evidence." There is a single case to support the claim to the privilege for mental health practitioners in the absence of a specific law granting it. In that case, Judge Harry M. Fisher ruled: "I am persuaded that the courts will guard the secrets which come to the psychiatrist and will not permit him to disclose them. I am persuaded that it is just one of those cases where the privilege ought to be granted and protected."[8]

Judge Fisher's ruling was not appealed, though on the face of it one is led to speculate that a higher court would likely overturn his finding. There was no basis in Illinois law in 1952 for this finding that the psychiatrist-client relationship "ought to be granted" protection. In most states, such is still the case.

Mental health therapists of all kinds, who may happen to

be clergy as well, would probably be best advised to consider what protection is provided to therapists, rather than to clergy, as they seek to determine the scope of protection afforded their communications with patients or clients.

Military Chaplains. The foundation for the privilege in connection with the military chaplaincy is found in the *Manual for Courts Martial,* Rule 503:

(a) *General rule of privilege.* A person has a privilege to refuse to disclose and to prevent another from disclosing a confidential communication by the person to a clergyman or to a clergyman's assistant, if such communication is made either as a formal act of religion or as a matter of conscience.

(b) *Definitions.* As used in this rule:
(1) A "clergyman" is a minister, priest, rabbi, chaplain or similar functionary of a religious organization, or an individual reasonably believed to be so by the persons consulting the clergyman.
(2) A communication is "confidential" if made to a clergyman in the clergyman's capacity as a spiritual advisor or to a clergyman's assistant in the assistant's official capacity and is not intended to be disclosed to third persons other than those to whom disclosure is in furtherance of the purpose of the communication or to those reasonably necessary for the transmission of the communication.

(c) *Who may claim the privilege.* The privilege may be claimed by the person, the guardian or conservator, or by a personal representative if the person is deceased. The clergyman or clergyman's assistant who received the communication may claim the privilege on behalf of the person. The authority of the clergyman or clergyman's assistant to do so is presumed in the absence of evidence to the contrary.

For the most part this rule is based on the proposed Federal Rule of Evidence 506 (a), which was proposed by the United States Supreme Court but impounded by the Congress. It has continued to exercise considerable influence over the shape of confidentiality statutes and rulings since it was proposed. Federal Rule of Evidence 506 (a) also forms the basis for the Model Statute proposed by the National Conference of Commissioners on Uniform Laws/American Law Institute. (See chapter 12.)

There are some unique features of the MCM provisions, however. Note, first, that the military extends protection to *assistants* to clergy. This coverage has been an established rule in the military for a number of years in recognition of the special role of the chaplain's assistant. Only one state, Mississippi, allows any similar coverage in specific language and that law covers a minister's secretary. The only case law supporting such an extension is contained in *Verplank,* cited extensively elsewhere.

Note further that the MCM rule is applicable to statements that are handled by others in the course of being transmitted or translated. This provision recognizes the fact that the military setting often requires communications to be transmitted by third parties. If the communication falls into the hands of unauthorized third parties, not "in furtherance of the purpose of the communication or those reasonably necessary for the transmission of the communication" the confidential nature of the material is compromised.

It is also important to observe an implied privilege accorded to written records of the confidential communication contained in this section of the MCM rule. Especially in states where the older traditional statutes exist, and in many more recent laws, it is not likely that written records of confessions or other communications are so protected.

In these three aspects, the protection afforded military chaplains under Rule 503 appears stronger than that afforded by most civilian statutes.

The military rule is somewhat restrictive, however, in a

very crucial area. Its protection extends only to communications that are *"made either as a formal act of religion or as a matter of conscience."* The MCM does not define either of the operative clauses in this phrase. On the surface these threshold criteria would seem to eliminate most communications occurring within the context of marital counseling, for example, since such counseling is not a "formal act of religion" and only occasionally might involve some specific "matter of conscience."

It is unclear why the military has chosen this particular language. On the one hand it may be slightly less restrictive than the traditional "seal of confessional" language found in older state statutes. At the same time, there is no guidance as to what the language includes or what it is intended to exclude. Thus, the chaplain is left to use discretion and trust military tribunals to decide in each case what the language means.

In attempting to define the parameters of the rule, the army chief of chaplains' office has set out three possible interpretations.[9] The first is very restrictive, in which the privilege would apply to formal confessions given to receive absolution, after the manner of the old priest-penitent "discipline enjoined" laws. The second is very liberal, in which any communication with a chaplain would be considered privileged. The third, a "middle path," interprets "conscience" in its more generally accepted meaning and applies the privilege to a communication made out of a sense of right and wrong. This would seem to cover many communications that are not specifically "religious" in nature, but would still seem to exclude a great deal of marriage counseling from its purview unless the counseling was prompted by feelings of guilt or other "matters of conscience."

These three possible interpretations of Rule 503 have been reviewed by the assistant for military law of the Judge

Advocate General, who concluded that the "middle path" is the course which the courts-martial would most likely follow.[10] However, it should be noted that this opinion has no force of law. Since only one case in the military involved the clergy-penitent privilege[11] and it turned more on the staff officer role than on the clergy role of the military chaplain, there is virtually no case guidance on how a specific military court might regard the privilege in military courts.

There are special needs for a strong protection of the privilege in the relationships of military chaplains. Chaplains are called on to work in a totally interfaith environment, so they need to have confidentiality protected in ways not restricted to particular confessional practices. They are involved in a great deal of counseling, including marital and drug-related counseling—in areas that are more pronounced under the pressures peculiar to the military environment and that are growing rapidly. The privilege is needed to encourage full and frank communication concerning potentially embarrassing or legally culpable situations. In many ways, the current rules give coverage similar to that in the most progressive state statutes, as has been noted. In other ways, military chaplains are especially vulnerable under the current language of Rule 503.

In conclusion it should be noted that

—Chaplains may claim the protection described here only in military judicial proceedings, not in civilian courts;

—Communications, to be privileged, must occur with the chaplain in his or her capacity as spiritual leader, not his or her staff officer capacity;

—The communication must originate in a confidence that it will not be disclosed "except in furtherance of the purpose of the communication";

—The communication must be made as a "formal act of religion" or as "a matter of conscience";

—Waiver of the privilege is the right of persons making the communication, or their direct representatives, and given such a waiver the chaplain may be obligated to disclose the communication;

—Protected communications need not be merely oral but may extend to behavior, objects, and, in some cases, written or electronically communicated materials or information.

Institutional Chaplains. Prison and hospital settings that bring staff chaplains into daily contact with ill or dangerous persons present special problems in many aspects of ministry. Not the least of these problems relate to the issue of confidential communications. Like military chaplains, those serving in state and federal institutions serve in the dual capacities of spiritual advisor and institutional staff person. This duality is especially visible in the prison situation.

A case in point was reported in *The New York Times,* December 12, 1982. According to this report Chaplain Joel Lundak, an Episcopal priest serving as chaplain at the Nebraska Diagnostic and Evaluation Center, told prison officials that inmate Jon E. Esslinger had confessed to a double murder. Esslinger told the chaplain during a private conversation in the chaplain's office about having killed two young men in South Dakota the previous summer. Esslinger told Associated Press that he was not aware that Lundak would "pass on what I tell him," but Lundak contends that he warned the prisoner that information that affected the safety of others would not be considered confidential.

The conversation was not in the nature of a sacramental confession, and Lundak told me that he would not agree to hear a sacramental confession in the prison setting. He has been chaplain at the center for three years and is approved by the national clearinghouse of The Episcopal Church to serve as an institutional chaplain. He has a master's degree in counseling psychology.

After being told of the murders, Lundak urged Esslinger to assume responsibility for turning himself in but the prisoner refused. Lundak then spoke with the warden at the center, indicating only that a prisoner had confessed to committing a serious crime and had asked for advice. The warden then told the chaplain that he was under no legal or moral obligation to reveal the content of the conversation, but should do as he felt he should. Following that conversation, the chaplain made a full report to authorities, and Esslinger was indicted by a grand jury in South Dakota and at this writing is awaiting extradition from Nebraska to stand trial. Lundak was not called by the grand jury, but the South Dakota State's Attorney is considering calling him to testify in a future trial.

Lundak told the Associated Press, "I am always a priest. This is a rare event, a thing that puts any clergyman in a tight spot. . . . There was a young man here, suicidal, torn apart by what had happened. There were two young men—one of them just a boy—lying dead in a field somewhere. Their families were grieving; a decision had to be made."

Bishop James Warner told the Associated Press that he would investigate the action on behalf of the Episcopal Diocese of Nebraska, but no disciplinary action has been contemplated against Lundak. The state corrections officials support the chaplain, believing he acted properly. Lundak, confessing that his decision was not made lightly, continues to believe it was the proper course under the circumstances.

But was his decision proper? This case illustrates the dilemma of an institutional chaplain in the clearest possible terms, but in this case we must ask whether Lundak's behavior does serious harm to the principle of confidential communication with chaplains. If every minister, priest, or rabbi took this course in resolving the personal tensions and the ethical or spiritual problems presented in the confidential relationships we encounter (even when the confidences are not in the form of a sacramental confession), there would be little left of the principle—and much less reason for troubled persons to seek the counsel of spiritual advisors in the certainty that the clergy can be trusted with the secrets of troubled souls.

Chapter XV / SOME SPECIAL ETHICAL QUESTIONS

Are there some circumstances in which the exercise of the claim to privilege for certain conversations present clergy with ethical or moral dilemmas? What should the pastor do when faced with a choice of violating a confidence or risking the possibility that a confidant will do violence to another person? Should a minister allow himself or herself to be used for purposes of national security, when fellow workers are not aware of this role? What is the minister to do when he or she gains the trust of an unpopular or oppressed group in society, and then finds his or her position subject to manipulation by officials who want information or access to the group?

These are a few of the ethical questions presented in particular situations as the clergy weigh their responsibilities.

Is There a Duty to Warn? In 1968 a young man named Poddar met a young woman named Tanya. Both were students at the University of California at Berkeley. They dated often, but Poddar took the relationship more seriously than Tanya did, and she eventually rejected him. Poddar underwent severe emotional stress for which he received treatment by a psychologist. In the course of his therapy Poddar threatened to kill Tanya, and the psychologist took the threat seriously. The therapist reported the

matter to the police, who arrested Poddar briefly but
eventually released him. On the authority of a psychiatrist
who was his superior, the psychologist took no further steps
to apprise anyone else of the threat against Tanya's life.

Later, Poddar murdered Tanya. The girl's parents sued
the psychologist and others for negligence in their failure to
warn Tanya or someone who might have protected her. The
suit eventually came to the California Supreme Court on
appeal.[1] In its 5-2 final decision the court held that when a
therapist predicts that a patient represents an actual danger
to a third party, the therapist has a duty to warn that person
of the danger. A plurality of the judges of the court went
further, stating that if a therapist *should have* made such a
prediction (even if he or she did not actually do so), "he
bears a duty to exercise reasonable care to protect the
foreseeable victim of that danger."[2] The court stated: "In
this risk-infested society we can hardly tolerate the further
exposure to danger that would result from a concealed
knowledge of the therapist that his patient was lethal."[3]

The primary argument against the acceptance of this
"duty to warn," of course, is that it constitutes a breach of
confidentiality protected under statute. This danger to a
privileged relationship might serve to deter others from
seeking adequate treatment or cause those who do seek
treatment to be less than candid with the therapist and
thereby render the therapy ineffective.

In another California case the court rejected a contention
by the parents of a girl who committed suicide that the
psychiatrist in the case had "a duty . . . to breach the
confidence of doctor-patient relationship by revealing to
[the parents] disclosures made by their daughter about
conditions that might cause her to commit suicide." The
court held that the therapist is required to disclose the
contents of a confidential communication only when there is

the risk of a violent assault on a third party—not when the danger is self-inflicted harm or property damage.[4]

Some mental health therapists have a professional code of conduct which contains guidance on the "duty to warn." Unfortunately, the clergy does not have such codified guidance. Is there an inherent "duty to warn" in the pastor's relationship with those whom he or she counsels? If the pastor exercises such a duty, does this violate the confidentiality of the relationship? If they do not exercise this duty, are they negligently liable for the consequences? Within both the ethical and legal answers to such questions there is a great deal of ambivalence. Some would substitute the word *right* for the word *duty* in these questions, raising a different set of issues regarding the possession and exercise of the privilege.

There are standards of negligence in many professions. What is the standard of negligence for a minister? For us, there is not even a universal definition of the words *clergy, minister,* or *pastoral counselor.* There are references in common law and in statutes to clergy and ministers, but such attempts have been made to define them have created more problems than they have solved. There are no general principles upon which a court might judge the clergy's performance of his or her duty to predict possible actions. Some states have attempted to define "pastoral counselor" in state licensure laws, but this is far from universal.

A further potential conflict arises for the clergy when they must both maintain the confidence of the confidant and protect themselves from liability for improper disclosure in exercising the implied "duty to warn." In those churches where discipline imposes the absolute seal, the dilemma is heightened, though the decision is made by canon law.

The quandary presented by this situation is not new. Earlier this problem was discussed in Lyndwood's "Provinciale" of 1679. (See chapter 4.) There, it will be noted,

Lyndwood left the matter unresolved, merely recognizing the dilemma and quoting authorities on both sides.

Articuli Cleri (enacted in 1315 by the English Parliament) specifically excludes high treason from confessions subject to protection under privilege. There is, apparently, at least this one precedent to support the notion of a "duty to warn" civil authority of a danger to its safety—a circumstance not cited by the California court. Still, the conclusion is not definitive.

Is there a duty or a right to warn? The questions are difficult and will persist in the conscience of the clergy, and perhaps in the courtrooms of the land.

The Clergy Informer. In 1974 and 1975 the religious communities of the United States were rocked by revelations that clergy and church workers were serving as informers for the Central Intelligence Agency and the Federal Bureau of Investigation. For example, one missionary in Central America had been receiving a stipend of ten thousand dollars per year from the CIA for more than two decades. As the revelations recurred, confirmation came from the president, White House legal counsel, and the director of the CIA that such arrangements have been established policy of the United States since World War II.[5]

President Jimmy Carter moved to put some restraints on such uses of religious workers in the United States and abroad. The Reagan Administration moved to loosen some of the reins on governmental intelligence units, however, renewing concern about the use and abuse of religious personnel. The dangers of a too-close working relationship with such agencies are many. Describing the dangers, one church leader told the Select Committee on Intelligence of the United States Senate:

> If the use of clergy, missionaries or church workers for intelligence gathering is allowed to exist . . . the essential

relationship of confidentiality between clergy and parishioners, priests and confessors, and missionaries and national
coworkers would be eroded. Again neither church nor state
would be winners.[6]

Most religious denominations and communities in the
United States now have policy statements forbidding or
discouraging such cooperation. No laws exist that regulate,
control, or forbid the practice. Rather, it is an area entirely
dependent on executive order of the president of the
United States. Attempts, as recently as 1980, to put legal
bounds on the use of representatives of organized religion
for domestic or foreign surveillance activities have met
strong congressional and administrative resistance. Such
use was defended by former director of the CIA, William E.
Colby, in a letter dated November 5, 1975:

> In many countries of the world, representatives of the clergy,
> foreign and local, play a significant role and can be of
> assistance to the United States through the CIA with no
> reflection upon their integrity or their mission.[7]

In opposing such use of clergy, Father Anthony
Bellagamba told the Senate Intelligence Committee:

> If the people know that a missioner could, under certain
> circumstances, reveal their confidences, it would undercut the
> ability to share at its most basic level. There can be no trust in a
> minister who could, either voluntarily or under legal mandate
> of the President, reveal information shared in human
> confidentiality or sacramental seal. . . . We . . . have a serious
> responsibility to educate our missioners to the most sacred
> respect for people and the most intransigent secrecy for their
> confidentiality.[8]

Every major mission agency in the United States has
adopted similar views. However, one person presented

divergent testimony to the Senate Committee, speaking during hearings in 1980 to determine whether legal sanctions should be set on covert use of clergy by the CIA. He was the Reverend Ernest Lefever, the person who was nominated by President Reagan to head the human rights office at the U. S. State Department but was rejected by the Senate following confirmation hearings. Mr. Lefever said:

> I believe that the United States as the leader of the Free World should have a foreign intelligence capability second to none. This means that we need the capacity for clandestine collection, counterintelligence, and covert action abroad, all of which requires secrecy and sometimes deception. . . . I believe that foreign intelligence is wholly compatible with the American ethic as long as its objectives are just and legitimate, the means employed are just and appropriate, and the probable consequences will advance the cause of justice, freedom and peace in the world. . . .
>
> A garage mechanic, a politician and a preacher should all have an equal right to be patriotic. All American citizens should be free to cooperate with the CIA, FBI, HEW or any other U. S. agency in the pursuit of legitimate national interests.[9]

Which is the proper perspective? Since there are no legal constraints, clergy are left to their own consciences and to the regulations of church agencies.

The issues involved are basically the same regarding the domestic intelligence scene, except that the attorney general of the United States is authorized by law[10] to issue guidelines on the FBI's use of informants and confidential sources. The following is a portion of the guidelines issued by Attorney General Benjamin R. Civiletti on December 2, 1980, concerning the use of any informant under an obligation of legal privilege of confidentiality:

> (1) A person who is under the obligation of a legal privilege of confidentiality . . . may be used as a confidential source only upon the express approval in writing by the Director [of the

FBI] or a designated senior Headquarters official, except that a field office supervisor may approve one-time receipt of information not collected at the request of the FBI where the particular information is unprivileged. . . .

(2) Any such person approved as an informant or . . . source shall be advised by the FBI that in seeking information from him, the FBI is not requesting and does not advocate breach of any legal obligation of confidentiality. . . .

(3) If, despite the advice . . . that privileged information is not requested or advocated, he offers to provide information that is privileged or arguably privileged, the offer shall not be accepted unless a field office supervisor determines that *serious consequences* would ensue to an individual or severe property damage. A report concerning such information and the circumstances that warranted its acceptance shall be promptly forwarded to FBI Headquarters. . . .

(4) Regardless of state law, the procedures of this section must be followed for any licensed physician, any person admitted to practice law in a court of a state, any practicing clergyman, and any member of the news media.[11]

When Laws Are Broken. What is the status of the privilege in situations that bring the clergy into contact with those who break the law? This question is touched on in several cases discussed already. For instance in People v. Phillips a priest was not allowed to testify who had given him stolen goods within the context of the confessional. There have been several recent and controversial developments in this area, however, that pose special ethical problems.

1. Child Abuse Laws. The case of Mullen v. United States, cited elsewhere, involved the testimony of a Lutheran minister to the effect that a mother had confessed to him that she had abused her child. The minister was compelled to testify in the U. S. District Court for the District of Columbia. On appeal, the U. S. Court of Appeals granted a reversal of the mother's conviction, based in part on a finding that the minister should not have been allowed to testify concerning her confession to him.

However, as things stand today such a decision as that one reached in 1958 would be unlikely in most jurisdictions. In 1962 child abuse was recognized as a clinically observable condition. Since then there has been a trend toward mandatory reporting procedures for all professionals who have access to knowledge about child abuse cases.[12] The first mandatory reporting law was passed in 1963 and by 1974 all fifty states, the District of Columbia, and Puerto Rico had enacted such statutes. In addition to becoming nationwide, these laws have been broadened in scope and purpose so that they are now most appropriately called "child protection laws."

Who must report suspected cases of child abuse? Originally, reporting statutes were limited to medical personnel, but in recent years the base of mandated reporters has been broadened considerably. Some states list as many as fifteen different groups or individuals who must report, and most laws contain the catch-all category of "any other person." Indiana, New Jersey, Oklahoma, Rhode Island, Tennessee, Texas, and Utah impose this universal requirement as the primary focus of the statute and either do not name specific groups or use them only as illustrations. Thus, in most states clergy are probably required by statute to report any case of child abuse that they know about.

How is the privilege affected by this requirement? In twenty states[13] all privileged communications statutes except the attorney-client privilege are abrogated. Clearly this situation places clergy in these states firmly on the horns of a dilemma. Should an abusive parent in one of these states approach a priest for confession and absolution, the priest is not only subject to subpoena should the matter come to court, but he is also actually required by law to take the initiative in reporting the incident. Thirty-three states impose a criminal penalty for failure to make the report, and two others provide for civil liability. (Some authorities contend that civil liability exists even without statutory authority.)

Only Pennsylvania and South Carolina exempt the clergy-penitent privilege from the general abrogation. Mississippi, on the other hand, makes the blanket stipulation that the act of reporting is "not a breach of confidence."

If a suspected case of child abuse proves to be unfounded, all jurisdictions provide immunity from legal liability if the report is made "in good faith." This provision, while of cold comfort to clergy caught in the legal tangle represented by these statutes, is intended to protect any person reporting a suspected child abuse incident that proves erroneous.

While there is no "typical" statute, the Arizona law is instructive because of its particular language:

> The physician-patient privilege, husband-wife privilege, or any privilege except the attorney-client privilege, provided for by professions such as the practice of social work or nursing covered by law or a code of ethics regarding practitioner-client confidences, both as they relate to the competency of the witness and to the exclusion of confidential communications, shall not pertain in any civil or criminal litigation in which a child's neglect, dependency, abuse or abandonment is in issue in any judicial proceeding resulting from a report submitted pursuant to this article.[14]

This statute is complicated. Note the language which refers both to *law* and to *a code of ethics regarding . . . confidences.* While clergy codes of ethics have only occasionally carried weight with a court regarding the privilege, this statute specifically abrogates even that small margin of protection. Also, note that this law deals not only with *abuse,* but also with neglect, dependency, and abandonment of children.

Clearly this trend in child protection legislation represents a considerable danger to the clergy-penitent privilege, even if it is narrowly construed to include only the seal of the confessional (which would most likely be the case in Arizona under a traditional statute, for example).

The only solution to the dilemma is in the legislatures of the several states, where it seems advisable for the clergy to seek restoration of the privilege where it has been abrogated and to exercise vigilance against abrogation elsewhere. Unfortunately, such defensive action may seem at first to put the clergy in a position of seeking ways to protect child abusers. Upon reflection it is clear that this is no more the case than the existence of the privilege generally makes the clergy defenders of any other sinner. Case law is filled with instances where clergy have been involved confidentially with those who have or may have murdered, maimed, raped, and robbed. Ohio recognizes this fact by exempting clergy from reporting gunshot wounds, if such a report would violate a privileged communication.[15] Existence of the privilege does not condone any criminal act. The emotionally charged cause of child abuse is not different in this regard.

Abrogation under child protection legislation represents the most assertive and widespread attack on the privilege in recent years. It could contain the seeds of a very dangerous precedent when other kinds of criminal acts gain the level of populist attention that child abuse has gotten recently.

2. Conflict Situations. One of the more celebrated cases of the past decade was that of the Reverend Paul Boe, a Lutheran minister who spent ten days with the embattled American Indians who occupied Wounded Knee, South Dakota, in 1973. He was cited for contempt of court and ordered to jail by a federal district judge at Sioux Falls after he declined to answer certain questions for a federal grand jury. As head of the American Lutheran Church's Division of Social Service, Boe was well known to and trusted by the leaders of the American Indian Movement. During the

Wounded Knee occupation he was invited into the Indian encampment by AIM leaders Clyde Bellecourt and Dennis Banks.

Clearly Boe's role there was not "confessional" in nature. Bellecourt and Banks were not "penitents." The American Indian Movement was not a parish or church, though it had financial and moral church support. Boe's testimony was sought by a grand jury, not in open court. (See chapter 16.) It seems likely that he did not hear any confessions of sin during his ten days at Wounded Knee. In his appearances before the grand jury he did respond to a number of questions about what happened there, obviously feeling that those questions did not violate any confidences. When asked to identify persons whom he saw carrying guns, however, he refused and claimed that to reveal the identities of individuals with whom he had associated would be a betrayal of confidences.

Briefs submitted by Boe's attorneys .put forth a strong constitutional argument for the clergy privilege. They contended that religious groups are the only ones competent to determine the goals and purposes appropriate to the churches; that when a religious body deems confidentiality essential to the performance of the duties of its clergy, then the minister's refusal to violate that confidence is an "exercise of religion" protected by the constitution; and that only the most compelling interest of the state can serve as grounds for restricting that free exercise. Further, Boe contended that the information being sought from him was already available to the grand jury from sources not subject to the privilege and that in any case the jury was being used in an illegal manner to gather evidence against a person or persons already indicted.

Federal District Judge Paul Benson, himself a member of the American Lutheran Church, ruled against Boe and ordered him to respond to the grand jury's questions or go to jail. Boe faced the possibility of spending fourteen months in jail—the unexpired term of the sitting grand jury. Judge Benson's finding was reversed on appeal by the Eighth Circuit Court of Appeals. That court did not rule on the merits of the case or the constitutional issues presented to it, but found that Boe had been denied due process when he was not given adequate time to present a defense before Judge Benson found him in contempt. Boe was released, and the ruling was not appealed to the United States Supreme Court. The ending of the case of Paul Boe and the American Indian Movement is inconclusive, but it does raise a number of critical questions in situations where clergy find themselves dealing with persons in conflict situations.

Assessing the Boe case in *The Christian Century*, Dean Kelley wrote:

> At stake in the Boe case is an emerging relationship of great importance to society as a whole, but the "seal of the confessional" may not be the best image under which to understand it. In protecting the "priest-penitent privilege" and extending it . . . to clergymen-counselors and their counselees, legislatures have shown sensitivity to a relationship they thought worth conserving—not just for the sake of individual counselees and certainly not for the sake of any or all clergymen, but because it contributes to the healing and the equilibrium of society as a whole.
>
> One of the functions of religion is to help people handle their anxieties, guilts, fears, rages, doubts, and despairs by enabling them to find ultimate meaning in their lives. One of the clearest ways in which this function is performed is the counseling relationship, in which a trained professional helps troubled persons work through such problems. . . .
>
> This does not necessarily mean to condone or conspire in criminal activities, since the effective counselor understands that deliberate violations of the law are serious and seldom the answer to any problems; they can be justified only in a few instances where the laws are unjust or where obedience to

them works a greater wrong than overt conscientious disobedience.

Kelley proceeds to prescribe the image of *chaplain*—"the bearer of the concern and compassion of Christians to special populations having special needs"—as being appropriate in defining ministries like that of Paul Boe's at Wounded Knee. He cites other examples of clergy who have served the "chaplain" role with oppressed or deprived communities: workers with migrant laborers, led by Cesar Chavez, and the Reverend John P. Adams of The United Methodist Church with the Poor People's Campaign.

Kelley proceeds to observe that if such "chaplains" can be made "retroactively into an agent of the prosecution" and compelled to testify against those whose trust they have gained, "it will not be long before clergymen are unable to gain access" to situations of social conflict. Kelley feels that religious organizations working with oppressed and deprived communities must adopt policies that require ministers to respect and preserve the confidentiality of the relationship.

Clearly, cases such as that of Paul Boe present particular problems and controversial questions to the religious communities, embodying relationships and communications that need to be protected if the credibility of the religious presence with oppressed and deprived groups in our society is to be preserved. There are no precedents in case law for the application of the privilege claim. This is one of the uncharted frontiers where religion and the law meet.

Chapter *XVI*/THE PROBLEM OF GRAND JURIES

"No person shall be held to answer for a capital or otherwise infamous crime, unless on a presentment or indictment of a Grand Jury. . . ."
U.S. Constitution, Amendment V

Of all of the questions related to privileged communications and the clergy none are more problematical than those that arise in the confines of the grand jury room where the principles of the First and Fifth Amendments to the U.S. Constitution collide head-on.

On the one hand, the historical development of the grand jury has brought tremendous inquisitorial and investigative powers to that institution. Those powers are guaranteed by the Constitution itself. Such powers are clearly intended to assure that the community is directly and ultimately responsible for its own peace and security. The grand jury represents the unfettered power of the citizenry to look into any matter it deems necessary to investigate. There need not be any allegation of criminal acts; there need not be a specific charge pending before the panel; there need not be a presumption that an indictment will result. The rules of evidence that hold in criminal or civil proceedings do not apply. Witnesses are not permitted to be accompanied by counsel, since the grand jury hearing supposedly is not an adversary proceeding where questions of guilt or innocence are to be adjudicated. Evidence that would be excluded from a trial—including hearsay, suspicion, or unsubstantiated reports—is admissable.

In short, witnesses called to testify before a grand jury have fewer rights and privileges than persons appearing before any other tribunal in our system of justice.

On the other hand, organized religion and persons working in it are increasingly involved in missions with issues, persons, and groups in our society which are likely to draw the attention of grand juries. They have included concerns for social justice, human rights, economic justice, civil rights, antiwar, and corporate responsibility, among others. We can expect continuing conflicts between the rights and powers of grand juries described above and the need for clergy and lay representatives of religion to maintain the integrity and confidentiality of their missional relationships.

One victim of this conflict was Pastor Paul Boe and his ministry with the American Indian Movement at Wounded Knee, South Dakota, a case detailed elsewhere. Boe spent time behind bars for refusing to answer certain questions for a federal grand jury. His eventual freedom was obtained on procedural grounds, not through any weakening of the basic law supporting the authority of the grand jury.

A more recent case involved two layworkers in the Hispanic Affairs Office of The Episcopal Church in the U.S.A. A federal grand jury thought they had knowledge of certain persons believed to be involved with terrorist activities. The women declined to answer certain questions, claiming that they had a privileged relationship on behalf of the church with the individuals of interest to the grand jury. The claim of confidentiality was rejected by the grand jury, and the layworkers were sentenced to jail by the federal court of the Southern District of New York.

Case law is currently averse to the claim of privilege in grand jury inquiries.[1] This applies to all privileges even including, under some circumstances, the explicit constitutional guarantee of the Fifth Amendment against self-incrimination. In such a case, a witness guaranteed immunity from prosecution loses the protection of immunity from self-incrimination.[2]

In *Branzburg* v. *Hays,* the U. S. Supreme Court held that a newspaper reporter could be required to testify before a grand jury regarding his sources of confidential information. This action by the high court regarding the rights of the press has served as precedent in lower courts to deny First Amendment privileges in religion cases. It may indicate the direction the Supreme Court would go in the event that it is asked to review an appeal of claim of religious privilege before a grand jury.

One attorney with extensive experience in cases involving subpoenas to clergy and church workers has offered some advice to church workers caught in the web of a grand jury. Eugene R. Scheiman says:

> strong argument must be made that any subpoena served upon those pursuing church work must meet the following minimum requirements in order to pass constitutional muster and in order to be compelling to those whose testimony is sought:
>
>> The government must clearly show that there is probable cause to believe that the church worker possesses information which is directly relevant to a specific probable violation of law.
>>
>> The government must clearly show that the information it seeks cannot be obtained by alternative means, that is, from sources other than the church or its worker.

The government must clearly demonstrate a compelling
and overriding need for the information.

This minimal showing by the government is, of course, not
the ordinary test required when the government seeks
testimony. However, we are not dealing here with ordinary
cases but with those that admittedly involve the First
Amendment. These cases should not be viewed solely as
dealing with the power and function of a grand jury, or with
the reach of compulsory process against assertions of
common-law privileges, but as cases involving the free
exercise of religion. Indeed when viewed in proper context, it
is little to ask that the government meet the minimal tests
outlined above before being permitted to intrude on ground
considered, except in extraordinary cases, inviolate for as
long as this nation has existed.[3]

This is sound advice, but it cannot conceal the stark reality
of the moment. Those who find themselves subpoenaed to
appear before a grand jury will find little protection in case
law. However, each case represents a new opportunity to
assert First Amendment rights. Who can know at what point
a particular set of circumstances might produce new rulings
more responsive to the religious rights of clergy and those
they serve?

Still, the seriousness of the case can hardly be overstated.
The usual penalty for refusing to answer questions before a
grand jury is incarceration for the life of the particular jury
or until the witness agrees to testify. It is not unusual for
recalcitrant witnesses to spend months in jail, and some have
stayed more than a year. No clergy have met such treatment,
and it seems likely that should this occur in a case involving
confidential communications, the storm of public protest
might be intense. What effect the reaction would have on a
federal district judge in any particular case is unknown, of
course.

The grand jury represents particularly serious problems for clergy who may be called to testify about matters confidentially communicated in the course of the exercise of ministry. Protecting the seal of confidentiality could be costly.

(Only Michigan provides statutory privilege for clergy appearing before a grand jury.)

Chapter XVII / UNRESOLVED ISSUES NEEDING ATTENTION

What remains to be done to help the church and its ministers obtain the right to silence? Of course, pastors and church bodies can work for statutes granting them the right in those states which have no relevant laws in this field. State councils of churches seem the best channels, since they represent a large section of the religious community. Where possible, the effort should be a joint one, with Protestants, Catholics, and Jews participating.

But there are still many unresolved issues in this whole area of privileged communications which need the attention of the best theological and legal minds of the church before any really adequate statutes can become law.

Communications Involving a Third Person. The courts have sometimes held that where a third person is in some way involved in a confidential communication it cannot be considered privileged. Yet it seems that such an attitude can lead to obvious injustice which is against public good. For instance, the fact that a third person may accidentally or purposely overhear a confidential communication to a minister does not to any degree alter the intent or value of this communication. It was made with the understanding by the penitent that it was to remain confidential; it was received in the same spirit by the pastor. For the courts to allow a third party to reveal it or to rule that the two participants must now bring it out into the open seems contrary to the very purpose of granting the privilege. Rather, it would seem that the courts should demand that the third party not be allowed to reveal it and that the party should consider himself or herself under the same seal of secrecy as the two participating parties. Yet, under most present judicial practice, if a third party in any way overhears such a conversation, the communication is considered not privileged. It seems to this investigator that the courts need to reexamine the issues involved in the present legal practice and determine whether justice is really being served by refusing to recognize as privileged those communications overheard by a third party.

The courts need also to make clear the status of a penitential communication communicated to a third party. Under the attorney-client privilege, a communication shared by joint counsel or given to a lawyer's secretary for recording is still considered privileged. Normally, a physician's nurse cannot be made to testify to confidential information received by her from the physician concerning a patient's condition. But the courts do not seem to have clarified the status of persons associated with a pastor who might normally have access to confidential communications made to him or her. Examples of this would be other professional staff members of the church he serves, such as an associate or assistant pastor or a director of religious education, as well as a secretary. This investigator believes that these people should not be required to testify about confidential communications to which they had access, but there seems to be no clear assurance of this under present practice. The increasing number of multiple-staff churches makes it desirable that all staff members who are a party to a confidential communication be protected from revealing it.

Status of Communications from Married Couples. Another area still unresolved, at least from the point of view of the church, is the status of confidential communications received by a pastor during marriage counseling. Essentially, this is a case where a third party is involved, and such communications have not always been recognized as privileged. Yet, the very nature of this counseling demands that it be confidential if it is to be successful. Most ministers spend a substantial proportion of their time in this kind of counseling. To consider it not privileged in the eyes of the courts is to rob it of its potential effectiveness. Couples contemplating divorce or experiencing serious marital difficulties must be able to speak freely to the minister and to each other, in the presence of the minister, about whatever is contributing to the breakup of the marriage. In some instances acts which are considered criminal offenses by the state are revealed. Yet, their very revelation in the confidential confines of the pastor's study, the asking of forgiveness for them, the assurance of pardon in Christ's name spoken by the minister and accepted by both parties, and the subsequent atmosphere of honesty between the partners of the marriage may be the only way in which the union can be held together. For the courts to block the possibility of this complete honesty is not only ethically questionable but surely against good public policy. The legislatures of the several states should take action to assure the protection of the law for this confidential relationship between a pastor and a married couple where it is not now protected.

Discipline Enjoined by the Rules and Practice of the Religious Body. Many of the statutes granting the priest-penitent privilege require that to be privileged, statements must be made to clergy in their professional capacity *in the course of discipline enjoined by the rules and practice of the religious body to which they belong.* The courts have had no problem defining what this means for a Roman Catholic priest because his church has formal confession as a part of its rules and practice. But the problem becomes more difficult where rabbis and ministers are involved. In most Protestant denominations confession is not a sacrament of the church nor even a formal ordinance. Some recognize it and enjoin it upon their members on a voluntary basis; others do not mention it at all in their adopted standards of doctrine or worship. Yet, confession to a pastor is practiced at least informally by some members of nearly every denomination. How are the courts to decide if this confession was made in the course of discipline enjoined by the rules and practice of the religious body to which the pastor belongs? A statute worded in this way, and strictly construed, almost inevitably means that the courts grant the privilege to a pastor belonging to a denomination which formally recognizes confession as a church sacrament or ordinance and deny the privilege to all other ministers. In essence, such a ruling subjects the courts to the charge of religious discrimination and unconstitutional procedures. It would seem much wiser to word the present statutes granting the privilege in such a way that confession to a pastor is recognized as a practice of every religious body, however informally that confession may occur. Such a wording would save the courts from future embarrassment as well as grant equal privileges to ministers of every denomination in this country.

The Possession of the Privilege. In chapter 12 we discussed the issue of who really possesses the privilege in the priest-penitent relationship. Is it the penitents, as the courts have almost unanimously held, by virtue of the fact that they initiate the penitential communication and only they can give permission for it to be revealed? Or does the very sharing of the confidence also imply a sharing of the possession of the privilege, so that each party now has mutual responsibility for it? Under the laws of the Roman Catholic Church, a priest is allowed to reveal the contents of a confession in a court of law if the penitent first reveals to the court what he or she confessed to the priest and gives the priest permission to verify it. The contents of the communication under these circumstances are considered to be outside the confessional chamber and no longer secret. In substance, this practice affirms that the privilege belongs to the penitent. But such a solution may be too simple. For one thing, privileged communication always involves two-way communication. The penitent confesses to or confides in the pastor. The pastor, in turn, speaks also to the penitent. What the pastor says may, at times, deserve the same protection of secrecy as the communication of the penitent. Why, then, have the courts not been consistent and recognized that the pastor also now shares in the ultimate possession of the privilege? It seems to this investigator that logical consistency would demand this concession. After all, it would be very difficult to bring out the contents of a confession in a court of law without in some way also revealing what was said by the pastor to the penitent. Under the present legal standards, pastors can do nothing to protect themselves from these revelations, for once the penitent renounces the privilege, the contents of the whole communication are admissible as evidence. Simple justice would seem to demand that the pastors have some voice in determining whether a confidential conversation between themselves and their penitents could be admitted for testimony.

Another and perhaps more basic factor is also present— the protection of the innocent. In so many confessions of guilt made to a pastor, innocent parties are somehow involved. For these revelations to come out into the open would subject these third parties to slander or scandal and much grief. Under such circumstances, pastors as a matter of public policy should do all they can to prevent such open disclosures. But present legal practice ties their hands. If the guilty party wants to bring the whole scandal into the open, the pastor is powerless to stop this from happening. It would seem that the courts have a responsibility here to protect the innocent. They should recognize that pastors share the privilege of this communication and should not let it be revealed openly without their permission, based on their own judgment. Such actions could go a long way toward preventing injustice.

Despite the seeming logic in granting the ultimate possession of the privilege to the penitent, this action may be against public interest. More thought should be given to this whole matter and, if advisable, steps be taken to give legal recognition to a mutual possession of the privilege by both priest and penitent.

Communications with Laypersons. Counseling by laypersons is a practice that is growing rapidly, especially in large evangelical Protestant congregations. It is viewed by its many proponents as an opportunity to involve members in the work of the church in a way that both fulfills lay ministry and takes part of the burden off the shoulders of pastors. It involves laypersons in caring relationships with other members of the community of faith. Half a dozen training programs for lay counselors have been developed, most of them by evangelical church leaders.[1]

It is not the purpose here to call the lay counseling movement into question or to promote it. Clearly the notion has a great deal to commend it, both theologically and pastorally. At the same time, certain questions are raised by the practice for our concerns here regarding privileged communications.

The most obvious, of course, is the question of whether

the relationship between the lay counselor and the counselee is privileged. There is very little case law that goes directly to this question, leaving us to speculate as to how courts might approach the matter. Speculation on what courts in general might do involves odds that no one in Reno would touch on a bet!

The *Nally v. Grace Community Church*[2] case contained allegations that went directly to the issues raised here, since Grace Community Church of the Valley has an extensive lay counseling program. Some of those counselors were involved with Kenneth Nally, a twenty-four-year-old seminarian, at the time of his suicide. Nally's parents sued Grace Community Church and made numerous allegations —the second count of which sought judicial review of the training, selection, and hiring of spiritual counselors by Grace Church. After nineteen months of litigation, the court gave summary judgment to the defendants (Grace Church) on all counts. Thus, the matter of lay counselors per se has not been tested in ways that set dependable precedents, though this case is still active.

More to the point is *In re Verplank*,[3] in which the court held that a draft counseling service rendered by non-clergy staff counselors under the direct supervision of a minister, acting in accordance with church-established policies, fell within the protection of the California clergy privilege statute. In this instance, the court found that the work of the lay employees "conform in a general way with a significant portion of the activities of a minister subject to the privilege." Judge William P. Gray saw "the relationship between Rev. Verplank and the other counselors . . . to be closely akin to the relationship between a lawyer and the non-professional representatives that he engages to assist him in serving his clientele."

A second rendering that points toward a possible protection for the lay counseling movement is found in the

case of *Reutkemeier v. Nolte.*[4] In that 1917 Iowa case,
communications made to ruling elders of a Presbyterian
church in the course of enforcing established church
discipline were found to be protected. (See chapter 12.) On
the other side of this case, however, we must consider *Knight
v. Lee,* in which the opinion of the court was based partially
on a finding that the communication for which privilege was
claimed was made to an elder and deacon of the Christian
Church (Disciples of Christ)—not to a pastor—and that such
lay officers are not protected by the Indiana statute.[5]

These cases indicate some of the legal problems that
should be considered in the course of planning a lay
counseling program so that any risks at law which the
program might present can be minimized. Before setting up
such a program church leaders should check state statutes
that regulate or license counseling services. Most such laws
exclude churches and employees of religious organizations,
but they may restrict use of the word *counselor* in ways that
could lead to malpractice actions or other liability for the
unwary. In addition, it is important to remember that the
key to legal protection may be in the nature and quality of
the direct supervision of lay counselors provided by clergy.
Supervision, guidance, and training are important considerations, according to the implications to be drawn from
Verplank and from *Nally.*

Further, the counselors themseves must be persons
capable of protecting and keeping the confidences entrusted to them and must work in settings that provide
absolute privacy. If the counselor violates the confidentiality
of a communication, even unintentionally or carelessly, the
breach may be irreparable and the content of the
communication become available for testimony in a court.

The intent of what has been said here is to indicate the
direction in which protection for communications with lay
counselors might go. It should be noted, however, that

another outcome is possible and quite likely, given the nature of most state laws and court practices. Courts might very well treat lay counselors as "third parties," to whom divulging confidential information results in the waiver of the privilege, another unresolved issue discussed earlier in this chapter.

In any case, there is considerable room to question whether courts in most states would honor any privilege claimed by or for lay counselors on behalf of persons with whom they have counseled. How would courts treat such work when undertaken by statements of policy adopted by judicatories or church authorities? The American Lutheran Church has a partial reference to this possibility, claiming privileged status for "those lay persons elected as an officer or as a member of national or district staff of this Church."[6] On the other hand, The Episcopal Church made no such claim for certain members of its national staff called to testify before a federal grand jury in New York, resulting in extended incarceration of two lay employees of the denomination's Hispanic Commission in 1977.[7] In its opinion, the court stated:

> The court is compelled to arrive at the conclusion that the work performed by the respondents herein, while perhaps performed under spiritual auspices, is primarily in the nature of social work. A social worker has no privilege with respect to his or her aid. . . . This court is not free to extend the cloak of priest-penitent privilege so far as to cover persons engaged in social work simply because the Hispanic Commission is affiliated with a religious organization.

Would the court rule otherwise if lay employees or volunteers of a church or religious organization engaged in counseling or therapy? The issue is certainly unresolved at this time.

Clergy Malpractice Insurance? Do clergy need to be insured against professional malpractice? How is such insurance related to the matter of confidentiality of communications with clergy?

Clergy malpractice insurance was first introduced by a Wisconsin-based insurance company in 1968. Only one clergy malpractice case has ever reached the trial stage— *Nally v. Grace Community Church*, discussed above—and it was summarily dismissed by the Superior Court of California for Los Angeles County. Rumors of other cases have circulated for several years, but none have been reported in case law digests and a free-lance writer seeking cases for an article in *Liberty: A Magazine of Religious Freedom* found no insurance companies who had ever paid a claim on such a policy.[8]

There may be compelling reasons why clergy in particular circumstances feel they need to be covered by such insurance. From the perspective of privileged communication, however, at least one clear danger should be taken into consideration when the need for such insurance is evaluated. It is a well-settled point of law that an insured person can be compelled to cooperate with the insurer in defending a lawsuit for which a claim is made under liability insurance policies. In a clergy malpractice case, the testimony of the pastor, priest, or rabbi is almost certain to be crucial in his or her own defense. One attorney, who defended Grace Community Church in the case mentioned, says:

> In a case such as the Nally lawsuit, where the penitent/counselee is not available to testify, the defense may hinge on a clergyman disclosing confidential communications. If the clergyman refuses to make such disclosure, he might well be held to have violated the duty to cooperate with the insurer and release the insurer from his obligation to defend the suit. Thus, malpractice insurance may not always be an answer in this new arena.

He warns, further, that "since clergyman malpractice inevitably deals with doctrinal, ecclesiastical, and spiritual issues, judicial review will force the courts into dangerous territory."[9]

In addition to this danger there are two areas of potential liability that should be kept in mind. (They are discussed in chapter 15.) What happens when the pastor becomes aware that the counselee is a danger to another person, when a threat of bodily harm is made? If the pastor decides to warn the other person, thereby violating the confidentiality of the information, he or she could incur liability for civil action. The counselee could sue. On the other hand, if the third party is actually injured and was not warned by the clergy, there is the possibility of liability. The injured party, or his or her agents, could sue. This happened in *Nally v. Grace Church.* In such cases, the insurance might provide for legal defense. But at what price to the principle of the privilege?

There may be good reasons why clergy should consider purchasing malpractice insurance, but all of the factors involved should be taken into account in assessing its value.

Chapter *XVIII* / GUIDANCE FOR CLERGY

What steps should ministers take if they are subpoenaed by a court to give testimony in a case where the information they possess has come by way of confidential communications to them in their professional capacity? What guidance can be given them? The following suggestions might be helpful.

FIRST, they should secure a competent lawyer to advise them about the statutes of their state of residence which recognize the priest-penitent privilege. If the case is being tried in another state or in a federal court, they should discover what statutes might be applicable there. A majority of the states recognize the privilege and grant to the pastor some degree of immunity from testifying.

SECOND, the pastors should notify the church judicatory under which they serve that they have received the subpoena. They should inform the judicatory of the general nature of the case without divulging the confidential aspects of it. The steps they plan to take and the steps taken to date in responding to the subpoena should be outlined to the judicatory and its support requested. In most cases this support will be given readily, and it may provide added weight to their arguments before the court.

THIRD, they should appear in court on the date set and respectfully answer those questions of the court that are general in nature and that do not touch on the circumstances or contents of the confidential communication. They should take the oath of a witness as offered, unless they conscientiously object to it.

FOURTH, when the questions directed to them demand answers which they deem in their judgment to come within the bounds of confidential communications received by them or made by them, they should respectfully refuse to answer. If a statute is on record which grants them immunity from testifying to confidential communications, they should now claim the privileges of this statute. Under such circumstances, the court will normally excuse them from further service as a witness. If they are not protected by statute, they should still refuse to answer, knowing that they may be held in contempt of court and possibly fined or jailed or both. However, more is involved here than merely their personal inconvenience. At stake is the free practice of the sacraments or ordinances of the faith they profess. The harm they would do to the cause of Christianity by breaking the seal of confession would be considerably greater than any harm which might come to them.

FIFTH, in a case in which they are not protected by statute, ministers should give the court some reasonable explanation for their refusal to testify. The court will have to decide if it will accept their reasons, but even if it does not, the pastors will have made their positive Christian witness to the faith they hold. Though clergy must, of course, work out their own line of argument, there are several points which might be helpful to bring out. One is that a formal oath in court ought not to bind a person to commit a sin. The Westminster Confession of Faith states that a person may not "bind himself by oath to anything but what is good and just." It also states that an oath "cannot oblige to sin."[1] One

Presbyterian minister who has given this matter some thought writes that on the basis of these statements of the Westminster Confession of Faith, his probable actions in court would be as follows:

> I might feel obliged to affirm that it would be "sinful" for me to make any public statements which would injure some person who had come to me in the relationship of pastoral care and spiritual guidance, which functions are a cardinal part of my obligation as a Minister of the Word and Sacraments. At this point I might stand upon the Confession, Chapter VI, vi, and the supporting Scripture texts there noted, to set forth the seriousness with which I take my responsibility to avoid what I believe to be a sinful act. I would also adduce other Scripture concerning the obligation of a Christian to the welfare of another to support my contention that it would be "sinful" for me to injure such a person as noted above.[2]

If the witnesses are convinced that their testimony in the case would be sinful acts, they should make this clear to the court. Very few judges would press the issue beyond this point, for most of them would understand that no minister could knowingly injure some person who had come for spiritual guidance. Furthermore, they would understand their Christian concern for the welfare of another person. On these bases alone, the pastors would probably be excused.

However, a second point which pastors could bring to the attention of the court is the one already discussed several times—the obligation of the state to assure the free practice of religious duties without oppression. The pastors might cite the United States constitutional guarantees on this point as well as any doctrinal standards of their own church which are relevant. The Presbyterian, for instance, could cite that section from the Confession of Faith which deals with the duties of civil magistrates in their relation to the church:

> Civil magistrates may not assume to themselves the administra-
> tion of the word and sacraments; or the power of the keys
> of the kingdom of heaven; or, in the least, interfere in matters
> of faith. Yet, as nursing fathers, it is the duty of civil
> magistrates to protect the church of our common Lord,
> without giving preference to any denomination of Christians
> above the rest, in such a manner that all ecclesiastical persons
> whatever shall enjoy the full, free, and unquestioned liberty of
> discharging every part of their sacred functions, without
> violence or danger. And, as Jesus Christ hath appointed a
> regular government and discipline in his church, no law of any
> commonwealth should interfere with, let, or hinder, the due
> exercise thereof, among the voluntary members of any
> denomination of Christians, according to their own pro-
> fession and belief.[3]

While a court would not feel bound to the doctrinal
standards of any particular denomination, most would
recognize that it is their duty to give pastors "full, free, and
unquestioned liberty of discharging every part of their
sacred functions." The ministers would then have to show
the court how the hearing of confessions and the giving of
spiritual advice and counsel are a part of their sacred
functions. They could bring to the court's attention those
constitutional standards of their church which prescribe this
as a part of the office of the ministry.[4] Most denominations
have set these functions down in some systematic order and
they are readily accessible to pastors. The court should
know how pastors see their role in relation to penitents who
come to them, as well as their responsibilities to those who
seek spiritual advice and counsel. While the court would
have to decide if requiring testimony from pastors would
hamper their liberty in discharging their sacred functions, it
is hardly conceivable that a judge would be blind to spiritual
matters which are not the business of the court.

If pastors bring these two points to the court's attention,
they are not assured that they will be excused from giving

testimony, but they will have made their own positive
Christian witness to their responsibilities as pastors and to
the court's responsibilities for the church. Further arguments would accomplish little.

If the courts do not recognize the pastors' statements as
valid grounds for refusing to testify, and if they are
convicted of contempt of court, they still have a *sixth* step
open to them. They may appeal. Such appeals are usually
lengthy and even costly. Perhaps their denominations will
stand behind them and help finance their litigation. But the
pastors should not hesitate to appeal their case to the highest
tribunal. If a clear decision is not rendered in their case, the
issue is only more confused the next time it arises. It is our
opinion that part of the reason for the present confusion is
that some cases in the past have not been appealed high
enough to allow the Supreme Court to rule on the issues
presented. The temptation of pastors is to pay a small fine
for contempt of court and rid themselves of the bother and
worry surrounding the case. But at stake are such issues as
the church's understanding of the role of its ministers and
the state's understanding of its role in relation to the
churches of the land. Personal inconvenience cannot excuse
us from clarifying these issues as much as possible. Our
calling as pastors demands that we use every effort to
strengthen the church and her ministry to society.

Additional helpful material, too long to quote here, about
the behavior of clergy in the courtroom can be found in
Legal Issues in the Practice of Ministry by Lindell L. Gumper.[5]

Appendix/STATUTES ON PRIVILEGED COMMUNICATION TO CLERGY

Forty-nine states, Puerto Rico, and the Virgin Islands have some form of statute recognizing the privilege to clergy. A few listed here may have been changed since the publication of this book. If in doubt, check a textbook of your state's law on evidence.

ALABAMA
Ala. Code tit. 12, sec. 21-166

Confidentiality of Communications with Clergymen
(a) As used in this section, unless a contrary meaning is clearly intended from the context in which the term appears, the following terms have the respective meanings hereinafter set forth and indicated:

(1) CLERGYMAN. Any duly ordained, licensed or commissioned minister, pastor, priest, rabbi or practitioner of any bona fide established church or religious organization and shall include and be limited to any person who regularly, as a vocation, devotes a substantial portion of his time and abilities to the service of his respective church or religious organization.

(2) LEGAL OR QUASI LEGAL PROCEEDINGS. Any proceeding, civil or criminal, in any court, whether a court of record, a grand jury investigation, a coroner's inquest and any proceeding or hearing before any public officer or administrative agency of the state of any political subdivision thereof.

(b) If any person shall communicate with a clergyman in his professional capacity and in a confidential manner (1) to make a confession, (2) to seek spiritual counsel or comfort, or (3) to enlist help or advice in connection with a marital problem, either such person or the clergyman shall have the privilege, in any legal or quasi legal proceeding, to refuse to disclose and to prevent the other from disclosing anything said by either party during such communication.

ALASKA
Alaska Civ. Rule 43-h (3)

Confessor-Confessant Privilege

A priest or clergyman shall not, without the consent of the person making the confession, be examined as to any confession made to him in his professional capacity, in the course of discipline enjoined by the church to which he belongs.

ARIZONA
Ariz. Rev. Stat. sec. 12-2233

Clergyman or Priest and Penitent

In a civil action a clergyman or priest shall not, without the consent of the person making a confession, be examined as to any confession made to him in his character as clergyman or priest in the course of discipline enjoined by the church to which he belongs.

ARKANSAS
Ark. Rule of Evid. 505

Religious Privilege

(a) Definitions. As used in this rule:

(1) A "Clergyman" is a minister, priest, rabbi, accredited Christian Science Practitioner, or other similar functionary of a religious organization, or an individual reasonably believed so to be by the person consulting him.

(2) A communication is "confidential" if made privately and not intended for further disclosure except to other persons present in furtherance of the purpose of the communication.

(b) General Rule of Privilege. A person has a privilege to refuse to disclose and to prevent another from disclosing a confidential communication by the person to a clergyman in his professional character as spiritual adviser.

(c) Who May Claim the Privilege. The privilege may be claimed by the person, by his guardian or conservator, or by his personal representative if he is deceased. The person who was the clergyman at the time of the communication is presumed to have authority to claim the privilege but only on behalf of the communicant.

CALIFORNIA
Cal. Evidence Code sec. 1033-1034, 1030-1032, 917, 912

Privilege of Penitent (Sec. 1033)
   Subject to Section 912, a penitent, whether or not a party, has a privilege to refuse to disclose, and to prevent another from disclosing, a penitential communication if he claims the privilege.

Privilege of Clergyman (Sec. 1034)
   Subject to Section 912, a clergyman, whether or not a party, has a privilege to refuse to disclose a penitential communication if he claims the privilege.

"Clergyman" (Sec. 1030)
   As used in this article, "clergyman" means a priest, minister, religious practitioner, or similar functionary of a church or of a religious denomination or religious organization.

"Penitent" (Sec. 1031)
   As used in this article, "penitent" means a person who has made a penitential communication to a clergyman.

"Penitential Communication" (Sec. 1032)
   As used in this article, "penitential communication" means a communication made in confidence, in the presence of no third person so far as the penitent is aware, to a clergyman who, in the course of the discipline or practice of his church, denomination, or organization, is authorized or accustomed to hear such communications and, under the discipline or tenets of his church, denomination, or organization, has a duty to keep such communications secret.

Presumption That Certain Communications
   Are Confidential (Sec. 917)
   Whenever a privilege is claimed on the ground that the matter sought to be disclosed is a communication made in confidence in the course of the lawyer-client, physician-patient, psychotherapist-patient, clergyman-penitent, or husband-wife relationship, the communication is presumed to have been made in confidence and

the opponent of the claim of privilege has the burden of proof to establish that the communication was not confidential.

Waiver of Privilege (Sec. 912)

(a) Except as otherwise provided in this section, the right of any person to claim a privilege provided by Section 954 (lawyer-client privilege), 980 (privilege for confidential marital communications), 994 (physician-patient privilege), 1014 (psychotherapist-patient privilege), 1033 (privilege of penitent), or 1034 (privilege of clergyman) is waived with respect to a communication protected by such privilege if any holder of the privilege, without coercion, has disclosed a significant part of the communication or has consented to such disclosure made by anyone. Consent to disclosure is manifested by any statement or other conduct of the holder of the privilege indicating his consent to the disclosure, including his failure to claim the privilege in any proceeding in which he has the legal standing and opportunity to claim the privilege.

(b) Where two or more persons are joint holders of a privilege provided by Section 954 (lawyer-client privilege), 994 (physician-patient privilege), or 1014 (psychotherapist-patient privilege), a waiver of the right of a particular joint holder of the privilege to claim the privilege does not affect the right of another joint holder to claim the privilege. In the case of the privilege provided by Section 980 (privilege for confidential marital communications), a waiver of the right of one spouse to claim the privilege does not affect the right of the other spouse to claim the privilege.

(c) A disclosure that is itself privileged is not a waiver of any privilege.

(d) A disclosure in confidence of a communication that is protected by a privilege provided by Section 954 (lawyer-client privilege), 994 (physician-patient privilege), or 1014 (psychotherapist-patient privilege), when such disclosure is reasonably necessary for the accomplishment of the purpose for which the lawyer, physician, or psychotherapist was consulted, is not a waiver of the privilege.

COLORADO

Colo. Rev. Stat. sec. 13-90-107

Who May Not Testify Without Consent

(1) There are particular relations in which it is the policy of the law to encourage confidence and to preserve it inviolate; therefore, a person shall not be examined as a witness in the following cases.

(C) A clergyman or priest shall not be examined without the consent of the person making the confession as to any confession made to him in his professional character in the course of discipline enjoined by the church to which he belongs.

CONNECTICUT
Conn. Gen. Stat. sec. 52-146b

Privileged Communications Made to Clergyman

A clergyman, priest, minister, rabbi or practitioner of any religious denomination accredited by the religious body to which he belongs who is settled in the work of the ministry shall not disclose confidential communications made to him in his professional capacity in any civil or criminal case or proceedings preliminary thereto, or in any legislative or administrative proceeding, unless the person making the confidential communication waives such privilege herein provided.

DELAWARE
Del. Code Ann. tit. 10, sec. 4316

Prohibition of Examination of Minister of Religion

No priest, clergyman, rabbi, practitioner of Christian Science, or other duly licensed, ordained or consecrated minister of any religion shall be examined in any civil or criminal proceedings in the courts of this State:

(1) With respect to any confession, or communication, made to him, in his professional capacity in the course of discipline enjoined by the church or other religious body to which he belongs, without the consent of the person making such confession or communication;

(2) With respect to any communication made to him, in his professional capacity in the course of giving religious or spiritual advice, without the consent of the person seeking such advice; or

(3) With respect to any communication made to him, in his professional capacity, by either spouse, in connection with any effort to reconcile estranged spouses, without the consent of the spouse making the communication.

DISTRICT OF COLUMBIA
D.C. Code sec. 14-309

Clergy

A priest, clergyman, rabbi, or other duly licensed, ordained, or consecrated minister of a religion authorized to perform a marriage ceremony in the District of Columbia or duly accredited practitioner of Christian Science may not be examined in any civil or criminal proceedings in the Federal courts in the District of Columbia and District of Columbia courts with respect to any—

(1) confession, or communication, made to him, in his professional capacity in the course of discipline enjoined by the church or other religious body to which he belongs, without the consent of the person making the confession or communication; or

(2) communication made to him, in his professional capacity in the course of giving religious or spiritual advice, without the consent of the person seeking the advice; or

(3) communication made to him, in his professional capacity, by either spouse, in connection with an effort to reconcile estranged spouses, without the consent of the spouse making the communication.

FLORIDA
Fla. Stat. sec. 90.505

Privilege with Respect
to Communications to Clergymen

(1) For the purposes of this section:

(a) A "clergyman" is a priest, rabbi, practitioner of Christian Science, or minister of any religious organization or denomination usually referred to as a church, or an individual reasonably believed to be by the person consulting him.

(b) A communication between a clergyman and a person is "confidential" if made privately for the purpose of seeking spiritual counsel and advice from the clergyman in the usual course of his practice or discipline and not intended for further disclosure except to other persons present in furtherance of the communication.

(2) A person has a privilege to refuse to disclose, and to prevent another from disclosing, a confidential communication by the person to a clergyman in his capacity as spiritual advisor.

(3) The privilege may be claimed by:

(a) The person.

(b) The guardian or conservator of a person.

(c) The personal representative of a deceased person.

(d) The clergyman, on behalf of the person. The clergyman's authority to do so is presumed in the absence of evidence to the contrary.

GEORGIA
Ga. Code Ann. sec. 38-419.1

Communications to Ministers, Priests and Rabbis

Every communication made by any person professing religious faith, or seeking spiritual comfort, to any Protestant minister of the Gospel, or to any priest of the Roman Catholic faith, or to any priest of the Greek Orthodox Catholic faith, or to any Jewish rabbi, or to any Christian or Jewish minister, by whatever name called, shall be deemed privileged. No such minister, priest or rabbi shall disclose any communications made to him by any such person professing religious faith, or seeking spiritual guidance, or be competent or compellable to testify with reference to any such communication in any court.

HAWAII
Haw. Rev. Stat. sec. 621-20.5

Communications to Clergymen

No clergyman of any church or religious denomination shall, without the consent of the person making the confidential communication, divulge in any action or proceeding, whether civil or criminal, any confidential communication made to him in his professional character according to the uses of the church or religious denomination to which he belongs.

IDAHO
Idaho Code Sec. 9-203

Confidential Relations and Communications

There are particular relations in which it is the policy of the law to encourage confidence and to preserve it inviolate; therefore, a person cannot be examined as a witness in the following cases:

1. A clergyman or priest cannot, without the consent of the person making the confession, be examined as to any confession made to him in his professional character in the course of discipline enjoined by the church to which he belongs.

ILLINOIS
Ill. Rev. Stat. ch. 51, sec. 48.1

Immunity

A clergyman, or priest, minister, rabbi or practitioner of any religious denomination accredited by the religious body to which he belongs, shall not be compelled to disclose in any court, or to any administrative board or agency, or to any public officer, a confession or admission made to him in his professional character or as a spiritual advisor in the course of the discipline enjoined by the rules or practices of such religious body or of the religions which he professes, nor be compelled to divulge any information which has been obtained by him in such professional character or as such spiritual advisor.

INDIANA
Ind. Code sec. 34-1-14-5

Incompetency as Witness (Sec. 5)
The following persons shall not be competent witnesses:
Fifth. Clergymen, as to confessions or admissions made to them in course of discipline enjoined by their respective churches.

IOWA
Iowa Code sec. 622.10

Communications in Professional
   Confidence-Exceptions-Application to Court
No practicing attorney, counselor, physician, surgeon, or the stenographer or confidential clerk of any such person, who obtains such information by reason of his employment, minister of the gospel or priest of any denomination shall be allowed, in giving testimony, to disclose any confidential communication properly entrusted to him in his professional capacity, and necessary and proper to enable him to discharge the functions of his office according to the usual course of practice or discipline. Such prohibition shall not apply to cases where the person in whose favor the same is made waives the rights conferred.

KANSAS
Kan. Stat. Ann sec. 60-429

Penitential Communication Privilege
(a) *Definitions.* As used in this section,
(1) the term "duly ordained minister of religion" means a person who has been ordained, in accordance with the ceremonial ritual, or discipline of a church, religious sect, or organization established on the basis of a community of faith and belief, doctrines and practices of a religious character, to preach and to

teach the doctrines of such church, sect, or organization and to administer the rites and ceremonies thereof in public worship, and who as his or her regular and customary vocation preaches and teaches the principles of religion and administers the ordinances of public worship as embodied in the creed or principles of such church, sect, or organization;

(2) the term "regular minister of religion" means one who as his or her customary vocation preaches and teaches the principles of religion of a church, a religious sect, or organization of which he or she is a member, without having been formally ordained as a minister of religion, and who is recognized by such church, sect, or organization as a regular minister;

(3) the term "regular or duly ordained minister of religion" does not include a person who irregularly or incidentally preaches and teaches the principles of religion of a church, religious sect, or organization and does not include any person who may have been duly ordained a minister in accordance with the ceremonial, rite, or discipline of a church, religious sect or organization, but who does not regularly, as a vocation, teach and preach the principles of religion and administer the ordinances of public worship as embodied in the creed or principles of his or her church, sect, or organization;

(4) "penitent" means a person who recognizes the existence and the authority of God and who seeks or receives from a regular or duly ordained minister of religion advice or assistance in determining or discharging his or her moral obligations, or in obtaining God's mercy or forgiveness for past culpable conduct;

(5) "penitential communication" means any communication between a penitent and a regular or duly ordained minister of religion which the penitent intends shall be kept secret and confidential and which pertains to advice or assistance in determining or discharging the penitent's moral obligations, or to obtaining God's mercy or forgiveness for past culpable conduct.

(b) *Privilege.* A person, whether or not a party, has a privilege to refuse to disclose, and to prevent a witness from disclosing a communication if he or she claims the privilege and the judge finds that:

(1) the communication was a penitential communication and

(2) the witness is the penitent or the minister, and

(3) the claimant is the penitent, or the minister making the claim on behalf of an absent penitent.

KENTUCKY
Ky. Rev. Stat. sec. 421.210

Competency of Certain Testimony
(4) No attorney shall testify concerning a communication made to him, in his professional character, by his client, or his advice thereon, without the client's consent; nor shall an ordained minister, priest, rabbi or accredited practitioner of an established church or religious organization be required to testify in any civil or criminal case of proceedings preliminary thereto, or in any administrative proceeding, concerning any information confidentially communicated to him in his professional capacity under such circumstances that to disclose the information would violate a sacred or moral trust, unless the person making the confidential communication waives such privilege herein provided.

LOUISIANA
La. Rev. Stat. Ann. sec. 15:477-478, 14:403

Privileged Communications to Clergyman (Sec. 477)
No clergyman is permitted, without the consent of the person making the communication, to disclose any communication made to him in confidence by one seeking his spiritual advice or consolation, or any information that he may have gotten by reason of such communication.

Right to Exclude Testimony;
  Nature of Privilege; Waiver (Sec. 478)
The right to exclude the testimony, as provided in the three articles last preceding, is purely personal, and can be set up only by the person in whose favor the right exists. If the right is waived, the legal advisor, the physician and the clergyman, as the case may be, may be examined and cross-examined to the same extent as any other witness.

Abuse of Children; Reports; Immunity;
  Central Registry; Investigations; Definitions;
  Waiver of Privilege; Penalties (Sec. 403)
A. The purpose of this section is to protect children whose physical or mental health and welfare are adversely affected by abuse and/or neglect and may be further threatened by the conduct of those responsible for their care and protection by

providing for the mandatory reporting of suspected cases by any person having reasonable cause to believe that such case exists. It is intended that as a result of such reports the protective services of the state shall be brought to bear on the situation in an effort to prevent further abuses, and to safeguard and enhance the welfare of these children. This section shall be administered and interpreted to provide the greatest possible protection as promptly as possible for such children.

B. Any person other than the alleged violator reporting pursuant to this section in good faith shall have immunity from liability, civil and criminal, that otherwise might be incurred or imposed. Such immunity shall extend to participation in any judicial proceeding resulting from such report.

C. Any privilege between husband and wife, or between any professional person and his client, such as physicians, and ministers, with the exception of the attorney and his client, shall not be grounds for excluding evidence at any proceeding regarding the abuse or neglect of the child or the cause thereof.

MAINE
Me. Rule of Evid. 505

Religious Privilege

(a) *Definitions.* As used in this rule:

(1) A "clergyman" is a minister, priest, rabbi, accredited Christian Science practitioner, or other similar functionary of a religious organization, or an individual reasonably believed so to be by the person consulting him.

(2) A communication is "confidential" if made privately and not intended for further disclosure except to other persons present in furtherance of the purpose of the communication.

(b) *General Rule of Privilege.* A person has a privilege to refuse to disclose and to prevent another from disclosing a confidential communication by the person to a clergyman in his professional character as spiritual advisor.

(c) *Who May Claim the Privilege.* The privilege may be claimed by the person, by his guardian or conservator, or by his personal representative if he is deceased. The person who was the clergyman at the time of the communication is presumed to have the authority to claim the privilege but only on behalf of the communicant.

MARYLAND
Md. Cts. & Jud. Proc. Code Ann. sec. 9-111

Minister, Clergyman or Priest
A minister of the gospel, clergyman, or priest of an established church of any denomination may not be compelled to testify on any matter in relation to any confession or communication made to him in confidence by a person seeking his spiritual advice or consolation.

MASSACHUSETTS
Mass. Ann. Laws ch. 233, sec. 20A

Certain Communications to Priests,
   Rabbis, Ministers and Christian Science Practitioners
   Shall Be Privileged.
A priest, rabbi or ordained or licensed minister of any church or an accredited Christian Science practitioner shall not, without the consent of the person making the confession, be allowed to disclose a confession made to him in his professional character, in the course of discipline enjoined by the rules or practice of the religious body to which he belongs; nor shall a priest, rabbi or ordained or licensed minister of any church or an accredited Christian Science practitioner testify as to any communication made to him by any person in seeking religious or spiritual advice or comfort, or as to his advice given thereon in the course of his professional duties or in his professional character, without the consent of such person.

MICHIGAN
Mich. Comp. Laws sec. 600.2156, 767.5a

Minister, Priest, Christian Science Practitioner
   Not to Disclose Confessions (600.2156)
No minister of the gospel, or priest of any denomination whatsoever, or duly accredited Christian Science practitioner, shall be allowed to disclose any confessions made to him in his professional character, in the course of discipline enjoined by the rules or practice of such denomination. (Sec. 2156)

*Certain Communications Declared Privileged
and Confidential* (767.5a)

In any inquiry authorized by this act* communications between reporters of newspapers or other publications and their informants are hereby declared to be privileged and confidential. Any communications between attorneys and their clients, between clergymen and the members of their respective churches, and between physicians and their patients are hereby declared to be privileged and confidential when such communications were necessary to enable such attorneys, clergymen, or physicians to serve as such attorney, clergyman, or physician. (Sec. 5a.)

MINNESOTA
Minn. Stat. sec. 595.02

Competency of Witnesses

Every person of sufficient understanding, including a party, may testify in any action or proceeding, civil or criminal, in court or before any person who has authority to receive evidence, except as follows:

(3) A clergyman or other minister of any religion shall not, without the consent of the party making the confession, be allowed to disclose a confession made to him in his professional character, in the course of discipline enjoined by the rules or practice of the religious body to which he belongs; nor shall a clergyman or other minister of any religion be examined as to any communication made to him by any person seeking religious or spiritual advice, aid, or comfort or his advice given thereon in the course of his professional character, without the consent of such person.

MISSISSIPPI
Miss. Code Ann. sec. 13-1-22

Confidentiality of Priest-Penitent Communications

(1) As used in this section:

(a) A "clergyman" is a minister, priest, rabbi, or other similar functionary of a church, religious organization, or religious denomination.

---

*Editor's Note: The "act" referred to pertains specifically to grand jury inquiries.

(b) A communication is "confidential" if made privately and not intended for further disclosure except in furtherance of the purpose of the communication.

(2) A person has a privilege to refuse to disclose and to prevent another from disclosing a confidential communication by the person to a clergyman in his professional character as spiritual advisor.

(3) The privilege may be claimed by the person, by his guardian or conservator, or by his personal representative if he is deceased.

The clergyman shall claim the privilege on behalf of the person unless the privilege is waived.

(4) A clergyman's secretary, stenographer or clerk shall not be examined without the consent of the clergyman concerning any fact, the knowledge of which was acquired in such capacity.

MISSOURI
Mo. Rev. Stat. sec. 491.060

Persons Incompetent to Testify
The following persons shall be incompetent to testify:

(4) Any person practicing as a minister of the gospel, priest, rabbi or other person serving in a similar capacity for any organized religion, concerning a communication made to him in his professional capacity for the purpose of obtaining spiritual counseling, or absolution in accordance with a religious requirement. Any minister of the gospel, priest or rabbi, concerning a communication made to him in his professional capacity as a spiritual advisor, confessor, counselor or comforter.

MONTANA
Mont. Code Ann. sec. 26-1-801, 26-1-804

Policy to Protect Confidentiality
  in Certain Relations (Sec. 26-1-801)
There are particular relations in which it is the policy of the law to encourage confidence and to preserve it inviolate; therefore, a person cannot be examined as a witness in the cases enumerated in this part.

Confessions Made to Member of Clergy (Sec. 26-1-804)
A clergyman or priest cannot, without the consent of the person making the confession, be examined as to any confession made to him in his professional character in the course of discipline enjoined by the church to which he belongs.

NEBRASKA
Neb. Rev. Stat. sec. 27-506

Communications to Clergyman; Definitions;
 General Rule of Privilege; Who May Claim Privilege
 (27-506. Rule 506)
 (1) As used in this rule:
   (a) A clergyman is a minister, priest, rabbi, or other similar functionary of a religious organization, or an individual reasonably believed so to be by the person consulting him; and
   (b) A communication is confidential if made privately and not intended for further disclosure except to other persons present in furtherance of the purpose of the communication.
 (2) A person has a privilege to refuse to disclose and to prevent another from disclosing a confidential communication by the person to a clergyman in his professional character as spiritual advisor.
 (3) The privilege may be claimed by the person, by his guardian or conservator, or by his personal representative if he is deceased. The clergyman may claim the privilege on behalf of the person. His authority so to do is presumed in the absence of evidence to the contrary.

NEVADA

Confessor and Confessant Privilege (Sec. 49.255)
A clergyman or priest shall not, without the consent of the person making the confession, be examined as a witness as to any confession made to him in his professional character.

NEW HAMPSHIRE
Author's Note: New Hampshire is the first state to enact licensing legislation for pastoral counselors with special training as such, and, accordingly, there is one privilege provision for clergy in general and another for licensed pastoral counselors.

N.H. Rev. Stat. Ann. sec. 516:35, 330-B:15

Privileged Communications
 Religious Leaders. A priest, rabbi or ordained or licensed minister of any church or a duly accredited Christian Science practitioner

shall not be required to disclose a confession or confidence made to him in his professional character as spiritual advisor, unless the person confessing or confiding waives the privilege. (Sec. 516:35)

Privileged Communications. The confidential relations and communications between a pastoral counselor licensed under this chapter and his client are placed on the same basis as those provided by law between attorney and client, and nothing in this chapter shall be construed to require any such privileged communications to be disclosed. (Sec. 330-B:15)

NEW JERSEY
N.J. Stat. Ann. sec. 2A:84A-23 (Rule of Evid. 29)

Priest-Penitent Privilege (Rule 29)

Subject to Rule 37,[1] a clergyman, minister or other person or practitioner authorized to perform similar functions, of any religion shall not be allowed or compelled to disclose a confession or other confidential communication made to him in his professional character, or as a spiritual advisor in the course of the discipline or practice of the religious body to which he belongs or of the religion which he professes.

NEW MEXICO
N.M. Rule of Evid. 506

Communications to Clergymen

(a) *Definitions.* As used in this rule:

(1) A "clergyman" is a minister, priest, rabbi or other similar functionary of a religious organization, or an individual reasonably believed so to be by the person consulting him.

(2) A communication is "confidential" if made privately and not intended for further disclosure except to other persons present in furtherance of the purpose of the communication.

(b) *General rule of privilege.* A person has a privilege to refuse to disclose and to prevent another from disclosing a confidential communication by the person to a clergyman in his professional character as spiritual advisor.

---

[1]Section 2A:84A-29

Author's Note: This section provides for waiver of the privilege by contracting not to claim it and by uncoerced, knowing disclosure of otherwise privileged information.

(c) *Who may claim the privilege.* The privilege may be claimed by the person, by his guardian or conservator, or by his personal representative if he is deceased. The clergyman may claim the privilege on behalf of the person. His authority so to do is presumed in the absence of evidence to the contrary.

NEW YORK
N.Y. Civ. Prac. Law and Rules sec. 4505 (McKinney)

Confidential Communication to Clergy Privileged

Unless the person confessing or confiding waives the privilege, a clergyman, or other minister of any religion or duly accredited Christian Science practitioner, shall not be allowed to disclose a confession or confidence made to him in his professional character as spiritual advisor.

NORTH CAROLINA
N.C. Gen. Stat. sec. 8-53.2

Communications Between Clergymen and Communicants

No priest, rabbi, accredited Christian Science practitioner, or a clergyman or ordained minister of an established church shall be competent to testify in any action, suit or proceeding concerning any information which was communicated to him and entrusted to him in his professional capacity, and necessary to enable him to discharge the functions of his office according to the usual course of his practice or discipline, wherein such person so communicating such information about himself or another is seeking spiritual counsel and advice relative to and growing out of the information so imparted, provided, however, that this section shall not apply where communicant in open court waives the privilege conferred.

NORTH DAKOTA
N.D. Rule of Evid. 505

Religious Privilege

(a) *Definitions.* As used in this rule:

(1) A "clergyman" is a minister, priest, rabbi, accredited Christian Science practitioner, or other similar functionary of a religious organization, or an individual reasonably believed so to be by the person consulting him.

(2) A communication is "confidential" if made privately and not

intended for further disclosure except to other persons present in furtherance of the purpose of the communication.

(b) *General rule of privilege*. A person has a privilege to refuse to disclose and to prevent another from disclosing a confidential communication by the person to a clergyman in his professional character as spiritual advisor.

(c) *Who may claim the privilege*. The privilege may be claimed by the person, by his guardian or conservator, or by his personal representative if he is deceased. The person who was the clergyman at the time of the communication is presumed to have authority to claim the privilege but only on behalf of the communicant.

OHIO
Ohio Rev. Code Ann. Sec. 2317.02 and 2921.22

Privileged Communications and Acts

The following persons shall not testify in certain respects:

(C) A clergyman, rabbi, priest, or regularly ordained, accredited, or licensed minister of an established and legally cognizable church, denomination, or sect, when the clergyman, rabbi, priest, or such minister remains accountable to the authority of that church, denomination or sect concerning a confession made, or any information confidentially communicated, to him for a religious counseling purpose in his professional character; however, the clergyman, rabbi, priest, or minister may testify by express consent of the person making the communication, except when the disclosure of the information is in violation of his sacred trust;

(E) Division (A) or (D) of this section does not require disclosure of information, when any of the following applies:

(1) The information is privileged by reason of the relationship between attorney and client, doctor and patient, licensed psychologist or licensed school psychologist and client, clergyman or rabbi or minister or priest and any person communicating information confidentially to him for a religious purpose in his professional character, or husband and wife.

(4) Disclosure of the information would amount to disclosure by an ordained clergyman of an organized religious body of a confidential communication made to him in his capacity as such by a person seeking his aid or counsel.

OKLAHOMA
Okla. Stat. Ann. tit. 12, sec. 385
Okla. Stat. Ann. tit. 12, sec. 2505 (Rule of Evid.)

Persons Incompetent to Testify Enumerated (Sec. 385)
The following persons shall be incompetent to testify:
5. A clergyman or priest, concerning any confession made to him in his professional character in the course of discipline enjoined by the church to which he belongs, without the consent of the person making the confession.
6. A physician or surgeon concerning any communication made to him by his patient with reference to any physical or supposed physical disease, or any knowledge obtained by a personal examination of any such patient: Provided, that if a person offer himself as a witness, that is to be deemed a consent to the examination; also, if an attorney, clergyman or priest, physician or surgeon on the same subject, within the meaning of the last three subdivisions of this Section.

Religious Privilege (Sec. 2505)
A. As used in this section:
1. A "clergyman" is a minister, priest, rabbi, accredited Christian Science practitioner or other similar functionary of a religious organization, or any individual reasonably believed to be a clergyman by the person consulting him; and
2. A communication is "confidential" if made privately and not intended for further disclosure except to other persons present in furtherance of the purpose of the communication.
B. A person has a privilege to refuse to disclose and to prevent another from disclosing his confidential communication made to a clergyman acting in his professional capacity.
C. The privilege may be claimed by the person, by his guardian or conservator, or by his personal representative if he is deceased. The clergyman is presumed to have authority to claim the privilege but only on behalf of the communicant.

OREGON
Or. Rev. Stat. sec. 44.040

Confidential Communication
(1) There are particular relations in which it is the policy of the law to encourage confidence, and to preserve it inviolate;

therefore, a person cannot be examined as a witness in the following cases:

(c) A member of the clergy shall not, without the consent of the person making the communication, be examined as to any confidential communication made to him in his professional character. As used in this paragraph, "member of the clergy" means a minister of any church, religious denomination or organization who in the course of the discipline or practice of that church, denomination or organization is authorized or accustomed to hearing confidential communications and, under the discipline or tenets of that church, denomination or organization, has a duty to keep such communications secret.

(2) If a party to the action, suit or proceeding offers himself as a witness, it is deemed a consent to the examination also of a wife, husband, attorney, clergyman, physician or surgeon, stenographer, licensed professional nurse, licensed psychologist, a certified staff member or local health authority officer or employee on the same subject.

PENNSYLVANIA
Pa. Cons. Stat. Ann. sec. 5943 (Purdon)

Confidential Communications to Clergymen
No clergyman, priest, rabbi or minister of the gospel of any regularly established church or religious organization, except clergymen or ministers, who are self-ordained or who are members of religious organizations in which members other than the leader thereof are deemed clergymen or ministers, who while in the course of his duties has acquired information from any person secretly and in confidence shall be compelled, or allowed without consent of such person, to disclose that information in any legal proceeding, trial or investigation before any government unit.

PUERTO RICO
P.R. Laws Ann. tit. 32, sec. 1734

Privileged Matters
A person cannot be examined as a witness in the following cases:

(3) A clergyman or priest cannot, without the consent of the person making the confession, be examined as to any confession made to him in his professional character in the course of

discipline by the church to which he belongs; nor as to any information obtained by him from a person about to make such confession and received in the course of preparation for such confession.

RHODE ISLAND
R.I. Gen. Laws sec. 9-17-23

Privileged Communications to Clergymen
  In the trial of every cause, both civil and criminal, no clergyman or priest shall be competent to testify concerning any confession made to him in his professional character in the course of discipline enjoined by the church to which he belongs, without the consent of the person making the confession. No duly ordained minister of the gospel, priest or rabbi of any denomination shall be allowed in giving testimony to disclose any confidential communication, properly entrusted to him in his professional capacity, and necessary and proper to enable him to discharge the functions of his office in the usual course of practice or discipline, without the consent of the person making such communication.

SOUTH CAROLINA
S.C. Code sec. 19-11-90

Priest-Penitent Privilege
  In any legal or quasi-legal trial, hearing or proceeding before any court, commission or committee no regular or duly ordained minister, priest or rabbi shall be required in giving testimony, to disclose any confidential communication properly entrusted to him in his professional capacity and necessary and proper to enable him to discharge the functions of his office according to the usual course of practice or discipline of his church or religious body. This prohibition shall not apply to cases where the party in whose favor it is made waives the rights conferred.

SOUTH DAKOTA
S.D. Codified Laws sec. 19-13-16 to 18

Religious Privilege—Definition of Terms As used in sec. 19-13-16 to 19-13-18, inclusive:
  (1) A "clergyman" is a minister, priest, rabbi, accredited Christian Science practitioner, or other similar functionary of a

religious organization, or an individual reasonably believed so to be by the person consulting him.

(2) A communication is "confidential" if made privately and not intended for further disclosure except to other persons present in furtherance of the purpose of the communication.

Privilege on Communications to Clergyman (19-13-17. Rule 505b)

A person has a privilege to refuse to disclose and to prevent another from disclosing a confidential communication by the person to a clergyman in his professional character as spiritual advisor.

Persons Entitled to Claim Religious Privilege (19-13-18. Rule 505c)

The privilege described by Sec. 19-13-17 may be claimed by the person, by his guardian or conservator, or by his personal representative if he is deceased. The person who was the clergyman at the time of the communication is presumed to have authority to claim the privilege but only on behalf of the communicant.

TENNESSEE

Tenn. Code Ann. sec. 24-109 to 111

Clergymen—Communications Confidential—
  Testimony Prohibited—Waiver (24-109)

No minister of the gospel, no priest of the Catholic Church, no rector of the Episcopal Church, no ordained rabbi, and no regular minister of religion of any religious organization or denomination usually referred to as a church, over the age of twenty-one (21) years, shall be allowed or required in giving testimony as a witness in any litigation, to disclose any information communicated to him in a confidential manner, properly entrusted to him in his professional capacity, and necessary to enable him to discharge the functions of his office according to the usual course of his practice or discipline, wherein such person so communicating such information about himself or another is seeking spiritual counsel and advice relative to and growing out of the information so imparted.

Such prohibition shall not apply to cases where the communicating party, or parties, waives the right so conferred by personal appearance in open court so declaring, or by an affidavit properly sworn to by such a one or ones, before some person authorized to administer oaths, and filed with the court wherein litigation is pending. Nothing in this section shall modify or in any wise change the law relative to "hearsay testimony."

Penalty When Clergyman Testifies
  Contrary to Preceding Section (24-110)
  Any minister of the gospel, priest of the Catholic Church, rector of the Episcopal Church, ordained rabbi, and any regular minister of religion of any religious organization or denomination usually referred to as a church, violating the provisions of Sec. 24-109, shall be guilty of a misdemeanor and fined not less than fifty dollars ($50.00) and imprisoned in the county jail or workhouse not exceeding six (6) months.

Determination of Qualifications of Clergyman (24-111)
  It shall be the duty of the judge of the court wherein such litigation is pending, when such testimony as prohibited in Sec. 24-109 is offered, to determine whether or not that person possesses the qualifications which prohibit him from testifying to the communications sought to be proven by him.

TEXAS
Code of Criminal Procedure, Ch. 38, Art. 38:111

Communications to Clergymen. (a) In this article:
(1) A "clergyman" is a minister, priest, rabbi, accredited Christian Science Practitioner, or other similar functionary of a religious organization or an individual reasonably believed so to be by the person consulting him.
(2) A communication is "confidential" if made privately and not intended for further disclosure except to other persons present in furtherance of the purpose of the communication.
  (b) A defendant has a privilege to refuse to disclose and to prevent another from disclosing a confidential communication by the defendant to a clergyman in his professional character as spiritual adviser.

UTAH
Utah Code Ann. sec. 78-24-8
Utah Rule of Evid. 29

Privileged Communications (78-24-8)
  There are particular relations in which it is the policy of the law to encourage confidence and to preserve it inviolate. Therefore, a person cannot be examined as a witness in the following cases:

(3) A clergyman or priest cannot, without the consent of the person making the confession, be examined as to any confession made to him in his professional character in the course of discipline enjoined by the church to which he belongs.

Priest-Penitent Privilege—Definitions—
  Penitential Communications (Rule 29)
  (1) As used in this rule:
  (a) "priest" means a priest, clergyman, minister of the gospel or other officer of a church or of a religious denomination or organization, who in the course of its discipline or practice is authorized or accustomed to hear, and has a duty to keep secret, penitential communications made by members of his church, denomination or organization;
  (b) "penitent" means a member of a church or religious denomination or organization who has made a penitential communication to a priest thereof;
  (c) "penitential communication" means a confession of culpable conduct made secretly and in confidence by a penitent to a priest in the course of discipline or practice of the church or religious denomination or organization of which the penitent is a member.
  (2) A person, whether or not a party, has a privilege to refuse to disclose, and to prevent a witness from disclosing a communication if he claims the privilege and the judge finds that:
  (a) The communication was a penitential communication and
  (b) The claimant is the penitent, or the priest making the claim on behalf of an absent penitent.

VERMONT
Vt. Stat. Ann. tit. 12, sec. 1607

Priests and Ministers
  A priest or minister of the gospel shall not be permitted to testify in court to statements made to him by a person under the sanctity of a religious confessional.

VIRGIN ISLANDS
V.I. Code Ann. tit. 5, sec. 857

Priest-Penitent Privilege;
  Definition; Penitential Communications
  (1) As used in this section:
  (a) "priest" means a priest, clergyman, minister of the gospel or

other officer of a church or of a religious denomination or organization, who in the course of its discipline or practice is authorized or accustomed to hear, and has a duty to keep secret, penitential communications made by members of his church, denomination or organization;

(b) "penitent" means a member of a church or religious denomination or organization who has made a penitential communication to a priest thereof;

(c) "penitential communication" means a confession of culpable conduct made secretly and in confidence by a penitent to a priest in the course of discipline or practice of the church or religious denomination or organization of which the penitent is a member.

(2) A person, whether or not a party, has a privilege to refuse to disclose, and to prevent a witness from disclosing a communication if he claims the privilege and the judge finds that:

(a) the communication was a penitential communication and

(b) the witness is the penitent or the priest, and

(c) the claimant is the penitent, or the priest making the claim on behalf of an absent penitent.

VIRGINIA
Va. Code sec. 8.01-400

Communications Between Ministers
of Religion and Persons They Counsel or Advise

No regular minister, priest, rabbi or accredited practitioner over the age of eighteen years, of any religious organization or denomination usually referred to as a church, shall be required in giving testimony as a witness in any civil action to disclose any information communicated to him in a confidential manner, properly entrusted to him in his professional capacity and necessary to enable him to discharge the functions of his office according to the usual course of his practice or discipline, wherein such person so communicating such information about himself or another is seeking spiritual counsel and advice relative to and growing out of the information so imparted.

WASHINGTON
Wash. Rev. Code Ann. sec. 5.60.060

Who Are Disqualified—Privileged Communications

(3) A clergyman or priest shall not, without the consent of a person making the confession, be examined as to any confession made to

him in his professional character, in the course of discipline enjoined by the church to which he belongs.

WISCONSIN
Wis. Stat. sec. 905.06

Communications to Clergymen

(1) *Definitions.* As used in this section:

(a) A "clergyman" is a minister, priest, rabbi, or other similar functionary of a religious organization, or an individual reasonably believed so to be by the person consulting him.

(b) A communication is "confidential" if made privately and not intended for further disclosure except to other persons present in furtherance of the purpose of the communication.

(2) *General rule of privilege.* A person has a privilege to refuse to disclose and to prevent another from disclosing a confidential communication by the person to a clergyman in his professional character as a spiritual advisor.

(3) *Who may claim the privilege.* The privilege may be claimed by the person, by his guardian or conservator, or by his personal representative if he is deceased. The clergyman may claim the privilege on behalf of the person. His authority so to do is presumed in the absence of evidence to the contrary.

WYOMING
Wy. Stat. Ann. sec. 1-12-101

Privileged Communications and Acts

(a) The following persons shall not testify in certain respects: (ii) A clergyman or priest concerning a confession made to him in his professional character if enjoined by the church to which he belongs.

NOTES AND ACKNOWLEDGMENTS

I. Why Is There a Problem?

1. Transcript of *Ex Parte Ronald Paul Salfen,* Collin County, Tex., May 14, 1981, p. 28 ff.
2. *The English Reports,* vol. 175 (Edinburgh: W. Green & Son, 1930), pp. 933-36.
3. Edward A. Hogan, Jr., "A Modern Problem on the Privilege of the Confessional," *Loyola Law Review,* 6 (New Orleans: School of Law, Loyola University, 1951-1952), 3-4.
4. *Ibid.,* p. 4.
5. *Ibid.,* pp. 5-6.
6. Guttmacher and Weihofen, *Psychiatry and the Law* (1952), p. 272, quoted by David W. Louisell in "The Psychologist in Today's Legal World: Part II," *Minnesota Law Review,* 41 (Minneapolis: Law School of the University of Minnesota, 1957), 745.

II. Where the Clergy and the Law Meet

1. Killingsworth v. Killingsworth, 217 So. 2d 57 (1968).
2. Wainscott v. Commonwealth, 652 S.W. 2d 163 (1978).
3. Letter from Dr. Emil Swenson to William H. Tiemann, dated June 23, 1961. Used by permission. Also see *In re* Swenson, 183 Minn. 602, 237 N.W. 589 (1931).
4. Simrin v. Simrin, 43 Calif. Rep. 376 (Dist. Ct. App. 1965).
5. McGrogan's will, 26 Pa. D. & C. Rep. 2d 37 (1961).
6. Ball v. State, 419 N.E. 2d 137 (1981).

7. *In re* Williams, 269 N.C. 68, 152 S.E. 2d 31 (1967). It would be difficult to devise a hypothetical case to demonstrate how *not* to assert the privilege that actually occurred in this case. The proper time to claim the privilege is after being sworn, when specific questions arise concerning the content of conversations that are considered privileged. See chapter 16.

III. How It All Began

1. Max Thurian, *Confession* (London: SCM Press, 1958), p. 59.
2. Edgar J. Goodspeed, *The Apostolic Fathers: An American Translation* (New York: Harper & Brothers, 1950), p. 77.
3. Bertrand Kurtscheid, *A History of the Seal of Confession* (St. Louis: B. Herder Book Company, 1927), p. 45.
4. John T. McNeill, *A History of the Cure of Souls* (New York: Harper & Brothers, 1951), p. 95.
5. Kurtscheid, *A History of the Seal of Confession*, pp. 43-44.
6. *Ibid.*, p. 50.
7. Quoted by Max Thurian, *Confession*, pp. 61-62, citing Migne, *Patrologiae cursus completus* (Paris, 1846), vol. 54.
8. Kurtscheid, *A History of the Seal of Confession*, pp. 51-55.
9. *Ibid.*, p. 56.
10. *Ibid.*, p. 57.
11. McNeill, *A History of the Cure of Souls*, p. 117.
12. *Ibid.*
13. Kurtscheid, *A History of the Seal of Confession*, p. 87.
14. Richard S. Nolan, "The Law of the Seal of Confession," *The Catholic Encyclopedia*, vol. 13, 649.
15. *Ibid.*
16. L'Observatore Romano (English ed.), April 11, 1974, pp. 1, 12. The papal statement was made during an audience held on April 3.
17. English translation of the *Introduction to the Rite of Penance*. International Committee on English in the Liturgy, 1974; "Introduction," para. III, d.

IV. The Common Law Came Out of England

1. Nolan, "The Law of the Seal of Confession."
2. *Ibid.*
3. *Ibid.*
4. *Ibid.*

5. *The English Reports,* vol. 175, p. 934, citing W. M. Best, *The Principles of the Law of Evidence,* vol. 1 (Albany: Weare C. Little & Co., 1876), p. 596. (See also later edition of Best [Frederick D. Linn & Co., 1882], vol. 2, p. 991.)

6. A free translation from the Latin text in W. M. Best, *The Principles of the Law of Evidence,* vol. 2 (Jersey City: Frederick D. Linn & Co., 1882), p. 991.

7. Nolan, "The Law of the Seal of Confession," p. 650.

8. *Ibid.*

9. *Ibid.*

10. *Ibid.,* pp. 650-51.

11. *Ibid.,* p. 651.

12. *Ibid.,* p. 652.

13. *Ibid.*

14. Best, *The Principles of the Law of Evidence,* vol. 2, pp. 991-92.

15. *Ibid.,* pp. 992-93.

16. *Ibid.,* p. 993.

17. Nolan, "The Law of the Seal of Confession," p. 653.

V. Anglicans and the Right to Silence

1. *The English Reports,* vol. 175, p. 935.

2. McNeill, *A History of the Cure of Souls,* p. 220.

3. *The English Reports,* vol. 175, p. 935, citing Best, *The Principles of the Law of Evidence,* vol. 1, p. 596.

4. McNeill, *A History of the Cure of Souls.*

5. Nolan, "The Law of the Seal of Confession," p. 655.

6. *Ibid.,* p. 656.

7. McNeill, *A History of the Cure of Souls,* pp. 223-45.

8. John Henry Wigmore, *A Treatise on the Anglo-American System of Evidence in Trials at Common Law,* vol. 8, rev., John T. McNaughton (Boston: Little, Brown & Co., 1961), §2394.

9. Hogan, "A Modern Problem on the Privilege of the Confessional," p. 12.

10. News item in *The New York Times,* April 28, 1959.

11. *The Constitution of The Episcopal Church,* Article X.

12. *The Book of Common Prayer,* p. 446.

13. "Memorandum on 'Privileged Communications' in The Episcopal Church," The General Convention of The Episcopal Church, N.Y. (n. d.), p. 3.

14. *Ibid.,* p. 4.

VI. Luther Reforms Confession

1. Martin Luther, *The Babylonian Captivity of the Church, Works of Martin Luther,* vol. 2 (Philadelphia: Muhlenburg Press, 1943), pp. 177, 292.
2. Martin Luther, *Discussion of Confession, Works of Martin Luther,* vol. 1 (Philadelphia: Muhlenburg Press, 1943), p. 89.
3. *Ibid.,* p. 90.
4. *Ibid.,* p. 92.
5. Ewald M. Plass, *What Luther Says,* vol. 1 (St. Louis: Concordia Publishing House, 1959), p. 333.
6. *Ibid.*
7. J. L. Neve, *The Augsburg Confession* (Philadelphia: The United Lutheran Publishing House, 1914), p. 10.
8. McNeill, *A History of the Cure of Souls,* p. 188.
9. *Minutes of the Twenty-Second Biennial Convention of The United Lutheran Church in America* (New York: The United Lutheran Church, 1960), pp. 277, 758.
10. *Minutes of the Church Council of The American Lutheran Church* (Minneapolis: The American Lutheran Church, 1960), p. 16.
11. Constitution of The American Lutheran Church (Minneapolis: Augsburg Publishing House, 1981), Article 6.33.11, p. 59.

VII. Confession in the Reformed Churches

1. McNeill, *A History of the Cure of Souls,* pp. 195-96.
2. *Ibid.*
3. *Second Helvetian Confession,* chapter 14, quoted in Walter Lüthi and Eduard Thurneysen, *Preaching, Confession, The Lord's Supper* (Richmond: John Knox Press, 1960), p. 55.
4. John Calvin, *Institutes of the Christian Religion,* vol. 1, trans., John Allen, (Philadelphia: Presbyterian Board of Christian Education, 1936), p. 690.
5. McNeill, *A History of the Cure of Souls,* p. 199.
6. Calvin, *Institutes,* I, p. 694. (Italics ours.)
7. *Ibid.*
8. *Ibid.,* p. 695.
9. John Calvin, *Commentary on a Harmony of the Evangelists, Matthew, Mark, and Luke,* vol. 2, trans., William Pringle (Grand Rapids: Wm. B. Eerdmans Publishing Co., 1949), pp. 342-53.
10. McNeill, *A History of the Cure of Souls,* p. 209.
11. *Ibid.,* pp. 259-60.

12. *Liturgie de Genève* (1945), p. 345, quoted in Thurian, *Confession,* p. 22.

13. *Minutes of the One-Hundred-Second General Assembly of the Presbyterian Church in the United States* (Atlanta: The Presbyterian Church in the United States, 1962), p. 134.

14. *Minutes of the General Assembly of the United Presbyterian Church in the United States of America* (New York: Office of the General Assembly, 1981), p. 539.

15. *Minutes of the 121st General Assembly, Presbyterian Church in the United States* (Atlanta: Office of the Stated Clerk, 1981), p. 105.

VIII. Confession in the Free Church Tradition

1. Gunnar Westin, *The Free Church Through the Ages,* trans. Virgil A. Olson (Nashville: Broadman Press, 1958), p. 72.

2. William L. Lumpkin, *Baptist Confessions of Faith* (Philadelphia: Judson Press, 1959), p. 27.

3. *Ibid.,* pp. 33, 34.

4. Quoted by Henry C. Vedder, *Balthasar Hubmaier* (New York: G. P. Putnam's Sons, 1905), pp. 212-14. For a time Hubmaier exerted great influence on early Baptist scholars; recently though he has fallen into disrepute among them.

5. Ernest A. Payne, *The Fellowship of Believers: Baptist Thought and Practice Yesterday and Today* (London: The Carey Kingsgate Press, 1954), pp. 104-5.

6. Lumpkin, *Baptist Confessions of Faith,* p. 388.

7. *Ibid.,* p. 395.

8. *Ibid.,* p. 34.

9. 103 Ark. 236 146 S.W. 516 (1912).

10. *The Lawyers Reports, Annotated, vol. 1917 D (Rochester: The Lawyers Co-operative Publishing Company, 1917), p. 279. (See also pp. 278-81.)*

11. Payne, *The Fellowship of Believers,* p. 104.

12. Bear v. Reformed Mennonite Church, 341 A.2d 105 (1975).

13. "American Baptist Policy Statement on Privileged Communications," Minutes of the Executive Committee of the General Board, American Baptist Churches, U.S.A., June 19, 1978.

IX. The Jewish Experience

1. Rabbi Juda, *Chasidim,* 21, as quoted by Warwich Elwin, *Confessions and Absolution in the Bible* (London: J. T. Hayes, 1883), p. 192.

2. Rabbi Mordecai Waxman, "The Changing American Rabbinate," in *The American Rabbi*, ed., Gilbert S. Rosenthal (New York: Ktav Publishing House, 1977), p. 178.
3. Rabbi Harold Saperstein, "The Changing Role of the Rabbi: A Reform Perspective," in Rosenthal, *The American Rabbi*, pp. 163-64.
4. Krugilov v. Krugilov, 29 Misc. 2d, 17, 217 N.Y.S. 2d, Sup. Ct. (1961), *appeal dismissed*, 226 N.Y.S. 2d 931 (1962).
5. Simrin v. Simrin, 43 Calif. Rep. 376 (Dist. Ct. App. 1965). Happily the court found, however, that the rabbi had secured the express agreement of both husband and wife, prior to undertaking counseling with them, that the conversations would be held in confidence and that neither would call him as a witness in the event of divorce action. In light of this prior agreement, the judge did not allow the rabbi to testify.

X. The Churches Reexamine Confession

1. News item in *The Presbyterian Journal*, February 13, 1963, p. 4.
2. Lüthi and Thurneysen, *Preaching, Confession, The Lord's Supper*, p. 41.
3. Dietrich Bonhoeffer, *Life Together* (New York: Harper & Row, Publishers, 1954), pp. 110-22.
4. *Ibid.*, p. 112.
5. Dietrich Bonhoeffer, *Ethics*, ed. Eberhard Bethge (New York: The Macmillan Company, 1955, 1962), p. 334.
6. Lüthi and Thurneysen, *Preaching, Confession, The Lord's Supper*, pp. 42-43.
7. Paul Tournier, *Guilt and Grace: A Psychological Study* (New York: Harper & Row, Publishers, 1962), p. 202.
8. O. Hobart Mowrer, *The Crisis in Psychiatry and Religion* (Princeton: D. Van Nostrand Company, 1961), p. 190.
9. Thurian, *Confession*, pp. 149-51. (See also pp. 100ff.)

XI. Some Necessary Definitions

1. Henry Campbell Black, *Black's Law Dictionary*, 4th ed. (St. Paul: West Publishing Company, 1951), pp. 345-46.
2. *Ibid.*, p. 1581. (Italics ours.)
3. *Corpus Juris Secundum*, vol. 72 (Brooklyn: The American Law Book Company, 1951), pp. 951-54.
4. *C. J. S.*, vol. 15 (1939), pp. 638-39.

5. *Ibid.*, p. 639.
6. *Ibid.*
7. *C. J. S.*, vol. 72, p. 954.
8. Thomas M. Carter, "Professional Immunity for Guidance Counselors," *The Personnel and Guidance Journal*, 33 (November 1954), 130-35.
9. *C. J. S.*, vol. 97 (1957), pp. 738-40.
10. *Ibid.*
11. *American Jurisprudence*, vol. 58 (San Francisco: Bancroft-Whitney Company, 1948), pp. 259-77.
12. *Ibid.*, pp. 220-24.
13. *Ibid.*, pp. 232-36, 303-4.
14. *Ibid.*, pp. 298-306.
15. *Ibid.*, pp. 296-97.
16. Wigmore, *Evidence,* vol. 8, (1940), §2285. (See expansion in §2396.)
17. Charles M. Whelan, "Governmental Attempts to Define Church and Religion," *The Annals of the American Academy of Political and Social Sciences* (November 1979), 33, 45.
18. *Ibid.*, pp. 33-34.
19. *Ibid.*, p. 35. See Davis v. Beason, 133 U.S. 333 (1980).
20. Whelan, "Governmental Attempts to Define Church and Religion." See Torasco v. Watkins, 367 U.S. 488 (1961).
21. Washington Ethical Society v. District of Columbia, 249 F. 2d 127 (D.C. Cir. 1957).
22. Universal Life Church v. United States of America, 372 F. Supp. 770, 776 (E.D. Calif., 1974).
23. Whelan, "Governmental Attempts to Define Church and Religion," pp. 44-45.
24. *Ibid.*, pp. 45-47.
25. 41 Fed. Reg. 6073 (Feb. 11, 1976).
26. In re Murtha, 279 A. 2d 880 (N.J., 1971).
27. Knight v. Lee, 80 Ind. 201 (1881).
28. Reutkemeier v. Knolte, 161 N.W. 290 (Iowa, 1917).
29. In re Verplank, 329 F. Supp. 433 (D.C. Calif. 1971).
30. Royston Pike, *Jehovah's Witnesses* (New York: Philosophical Library, 1954).

XII. Communications to Clergy Under the Common Law

1. Wigmore, *Evidence,* §2394.
2. L. C. J. Coleridge, "Letter to Mr. Gladstone" (Life and

Correspondence, 1904, vol. 2, p. 364), cited in Wigmore, *Evidence,* §§2394-2395.

3. Wigmore, *Evidence,* §2395, citing Ernest Bowen-Rowlands, *Seventy-Two Years at the Bar; A Memoir of Sir Harry Bodkin Poland* (New York: The Macmillan Company, 1924), p. 218.
4. Wigmore, *Evidence,* §2394.
5. Hogan, *Loyola Law Review,* vol. 6, no. 1 (1951-1952), p. 13; Wigmore, *Evidence,* §2394.
6. Wigmore, *Evidence,* §2394.
7. *The Lawyers Reports, Annotated,* vol. 1917 D (Rochester: The Lawyers Co-operative Publishing Company, 1917), p. 279. (See also pp. 278-81.)
8. *Ibid.*
9. *The English Reports,* p. 934.
10. Wigmore, *Evidence.*
11. *L. R. A.,* vol. 1917 D, p. 279.
12. Wigmore, *Evidence.*
13. *The Irish Reports* (Dublin: Incorporated Council of Law Reporting for Ireland, 1945), pp. 515-25.
14. Wigmore, *Evidence* (1940), §2396, citing Jeremy Bentham, *Rationale of Judicial Evidence,* vol. 7 (Bowring's ed., 1827), pp. 367 ff.

XIII. Statutes About the Right to Silence

1. *North Western Reporter,* vol. 237 (St. Paul: West Publishing Company, 1931), p. 589.
2. *American Law Reports, Annotated, Second Series,* vol. 22 (Rochester: The Lawyers Co-operative Publishing Company, 1952), pp. 1152-60.
3. *Ibid.,* p. 1153.
4. *Ibid.,* p. 1154.
5. *North Western Reporter,* vol. 237 (1931), pp. 590-91.
6. *A. L. R., Second Series,* vol. 22, pp. 1152-60.
7. *Ibid.,* pp. 1154-55.
8. *Ibid.,* p. 1155.
9. *Federal Reporter, Second Series,* vol. 263 (St. Paul: West Publishing Company, 1959), pp. 275-81.
10. *A. L. R., Second Series,* vol. 22, p. 1156.
11. *L. R. A.,* vol. 1917 D, p. 280.
12. *A. L. R., Second Series,* vol. 22, p. 1156.
13. *Ibid.,* pp. 1157-58.

14. *Indiana Supreme Court Reports,* vol. 80 (Indianapolis: Carlon & Hollenbeck, Printers and Binders, 1882), pp. 201-6.
15. *A. L. R., Second Series,* vol. 22, p. 1157.
16. *L. R. A.,* vol. 1917 D, pp. 274-76.
17. *A. L. R., Second Series,* vol. 22, p. 1158.
18. *Ibid.*
19. *Ibid.*
20. *Ibid.*
21. *Ibid.,* pp. 1158-59.
22. *Am. Jur.,* vol. 58, p. 216.
23. *A. L. R., Second Series,* vol. 22, p. 1159.
24. *Ibid.*
25. *Ibid.,* pp. 1145-46, 1149-50.
26. *L. R. A.,* vol. 1917 D, p. 281. ·(See also pp. 278-81.)
27. *Irish Reports* (1945), pp. 515-25.
28. *American Law Institute, Model Code of Evidence* (Philadelphia: American Law Institute, 1942), Rule 219.
29. *Uniform Rules of Evidence* (Philadelphia: American Law Institute, 1974), Rule 505.
30. *Federal Rules of Evidence in Criminal Matters* (New York: Practising Law Institute, 1977), p. 210.
31. *Ibid.,* p. 197.

XIV. Specialized Clergy: Specialized Problems

1. N. H. Rev. Stat. Ann., sec. 516:35.
2. N. H. Rev. Stat. Ann., sec. 330-B:15.
3. Ohio Rev. Stat. Ann. sec. 2921.22, E (6).
4. Simrin v. Simrin, 43 Calif. Rep. 376 (Dist. Ct. App. 1965).
5. Letter from George E. Doebler, executive director, Association of Mental Health Clergy, Inc., December 9, 1980.
6. In re Lifschuts, 2 Calif. 3d 415, 467 P. 2d 557, 566 (1970).
7. U.S. v. Kidd, 2 CMR 713 (1955).
8. Binder v. Ruvell, 52C2535, Circuit Court of Cook County, State of Illinois, 1952, as cited in *Journal of the American Medical Association* 150 (1952), 1241-42.
9. This section is based on an interview with, and information provided by, Chaplain (COL) Israel Drazin, Department of the Army, Office of the Chief of Chaplains, June 1982.
10. Memorandum to Department of the Army, Chief of

Chaplains, from Brigadier General Lloyd R. Rector, Assistant Judge Advocate General for Military Law, dated 9 December 1981.
11. Kidd, 2 CMR 713.

XV. Some Special Ethical Questions

1. 118 Calif. Rep. 129, 529 P 2d 553.
2. Tarasoff v. Regents, 551 P 2d 334 (1976).
3. *Ibid.*, 347-48.
4. Bellah v. Greenson, 81 Calif. App. 3d 614; 146 Calif. Rep. 535.
5. Testimony of James E. Wood, executive secretary, Baptist Joint Committee on Public Affairs before the Senate Select Committee on Intelligence, United States Senate, Ninety-Sixth Congress, Second Session, *National Intelligence Act of 1980* (Washington: U.S. Government Printing Office, 1980), p. 322.
6. *Ibid.*, p. 290.
7. Cited in the testimony of the Reverend Eugene L. Stockwell, associate general secretary for Overseas Ministries, National Council of Churches, *National Intelligence Act of 1980*, p. 298.
8. Testimony of Father Anthony Bellagamba, executive secretary, U.S. Catholic Mission Council, *National Intelligence Act of 1980*, p. 316.
9. Testimony of Ernest W. Lefever, president, Ethics and Public Policy Center, *National Intelligence Act of 1980*, pp. 309-11.
10. 28 USC 509, 510, 533.
11. Benjamin R. Civiletti, Attorney General of the United States, memorandum dated December 2, 1980, "Attorney General's Guidelines on FBI Use of Informants and Confidential Sources," pp. 9-10.
12. Education Council of the States, "Trends in Child Protection Laws—1979" (Denver: Education Council of the States, 1980). This booklet is acknowledged as the source of basic background used throughout this section.
13. Alabama, Arizona, Arkansas, Delaware, Florida, Idaho, Kansas, Kentucky, Louisiana, Maine, Michigan, Missouri, Nevada, New Hampshire, North Dakota, Rhode Island, South Carolina, Texas, West Virginia, Wyoming.
14. Ariz. Rev. Stat. 13-3620 (1978-79).
15. Ohio Rev. Code 2917.44 (1961).

XVI. The Problem of Grand Juries

1. Branzburg v. Hays, 408 U.S. 665.
2. Hale v. Hendsel, 201 U.S. 43, 67.
3. "Grand Jury Subpoenas and First Amendment Privileges," *The Annals of the American Academy of Political and Social Science* (November 1979), 106 ff.

XVII. Unresolved Issues Needing Attention

1. See Gary R. Collins, "Lay Counseling Within the Local Church," *Leadership* (Fall 1980), 78-86.
2. Case No. 18668-B (Los Angeles County Sup. Ct.) Calif., March 31, 1980. Summary judgment for the defendants, October 2, 1981.
3. 329 Fed. Supp. 433 (1971).
4. 179 Iowa 342, 161 N.W. 290 (1917).
5. 80 Ind. 201 (1881).
6. Constitution of the American Lutheran Church, chapter 6, sec. 6.33.11, revised 10-24-78, p. 59.
7. *In re* Wood, 430 F. Supp. 41 (1977).
8. See Maury M. Breecher, "Ministerial Malpractice," *Liberty: A Magazine of Religious Freedom* (March/April 1980), 15-17.
9. Samuel E. Ericsson, *Clergy Malpractice: Constitutional and Political Issues* (Oak Park, Ill.: The Center for Law & Religious Freedom, 1981), pp. 16-17, 29.

XVIII. Guidance for Clergy

1. "Of Lawful Oaths and Vows," in *The Confession of Faith of the Presbyterian Church in the United States* (Richmond: John Knox Press, 1951), p. 134.
2. Letter from Dr. James A. Millard, Jr., Stated Clerk and Treasurer of the Presbyterian Church in the United States, January 31, 1962. Used by permission. The chapter of the *Confession of Faith* referred to in his letter is entitled: "Of the Fall of Man, of Sin, and of the Punishment Thereof." It contains this statement: "Every sin . . . doth, in its own nature, bring guilt upon the sinner, whereby he is bound over to the wrath of God, the curse of the law, and so made subject to death, with all miseries spiritual, temporal, and eternal."
3. "Of Lawful Oaths and Vows," pp. 138-39.

4. Dr. Millard suggests, for instance, that a pastor of the Presbyterian Church, U. S., cite "The Form of Government," chapter 10, sections 10-1, 2, and 4, as well as "The Directory for the Worship and Work of the Church," chapter 24, sections 224-1, 2, and 4, both documents being constitutional material. Letter of January 31, 1962. Used by permission.
5. Gumper, Lindell, *Legal Issues in the Practice of Ministry* (Birmingham, Mich.: Psychological Studies and Consultation Program, 1981).

SUBJECT INDEX

AUTHOR INDEX

249

CASE INDEX